Goodbye, Kant!

SUNY series in Contemporary Italian Philosophy

Silvia Benso and Brian Schroeder, editors

Goodbye, Kant!

What Still Stands of the
Critique of Pure Reason

Maurizio Ferraris

Translated by
Richard Davies

Published by State University of New York Press, Albany

© 2013 State University of New York

Originally published in Italian as *Goodbye, Kant!*
© RCS Libri Milano, Bompiani, 2004

For information, contact State University of New York Press, Albany, NY
www.sunypress.edu

Production by Eileen Nizer
Marketing by Anne M. Valentine

Library of Congress Cataloging-in-Publication Data

Ferraris, Maurizio, 1956–
    [Goodbye, Kant! English]
    Goodbye, Kant! : what still stands of the critique of pure reason / Maurizio Ferraris ; translated by Richard Davies.
        pages cm. — (SUNY series in contemporary Italian philosophy)
    ISBN 978-1-4384-4809-1 (alk. paper)
    ISBN 978-1-4384-4808-4 (pbk. : alk. paper)
    1. Kant, Immanuel, 1724–1804. Kritik der reinen Vernunft. I. Davies, Richard (Richard Brian), 1944– translator. II. Title.

B2779.F47313 2013
121—dc23   2012045702

10 9 8 7 6 5 4 3 2 1

Contents

List of Figures

Introduction

From Königsberg to Kaliningrad

Königsberg, where Kant was born and lived, is one of the many cities that changed its name after the Second World War. Then it was in Prussia; today it is a Russian enclave between Poland and Lithuania and is called Kaliningrad. Its passing in 1945 from German to Russian seems to mirror the return of Leningrad/St. Petersburg from Russian to German after 1989. And it helps us to realize, as if on a journey through time rather than space, how much water had flowed under the bridge, not only in history (which is obvious enough) but also in philosophy (which is often less so).

Prompted by the bicentennial of Kant's death, this brief essay aims to set out his revolution, the so-called Copernican revolution, with the same affectionate irony with which the film *Goodbye Lenin!* treats the Soviet revolution.[1] Just as in Kant, so in Wolfgang Becker's *Deutsche Demokratische Republik*, we find pickled gherkins and dilapidated Trabant cars mixed in with the ideals of a more secure and less unjust world, with the yearning for a totalizing refoundation of knowledge and morality.[2]

The spirit in which we proceed is thus quite different from that which, 150 years ago, drove Franz Příhonský (1788–1859), a pupil of the Austrian philosopher Bernhard Bolzano (1781–1848), to write a book whose title represents its program, *The New Anti-Kant*,[3] which itself tells us that it was not the first.[4] What I offer is not a *Newest Anti-Kant*. And the aim is not to desecrate a monument but rather, if possible, to scrape off some of the rust and give it back to the present day. I am convinced that a listing of the Trabants and gherkins that are to be found in the *Critique of Pure Reason* would be a way not to say what is living and what is dead in the Copernican revolution (who would dare to undertake so vast a task?), but to present from another—perhaps better-disposed—point of view a classic of philosophy that has become embalmed by the passage of time and its own success.

February 12, 2004
M. F.

1

Kant's revolution[1]

Why start a revolution

When he died at the age of eighty on the February 12, 1804, Kant was as forgetful as Ronald Reagan was at the end of his life.[2] To overcome this, he wrote everything down on a large sheet of paper, on which metaphysical reflections are mixed in with laundry bills. He was the melancholy parody of what Kant regarded as the highest principle of his own philosophy, namely that an "I think" must accompany every representation or that there is a single world for the self that perceives it, that takes account of it, that remembers it, and that determines it through the categories.

This is an idea that had done the rounds under various guises in philosophy before Kant, but he crucially transformed it. The reference to subjectivity did not conflict with objectivity, but rather made it possible inasmuch as the self is not just a disorderly bundle of sensations but a principle of order endowed with two pure forms of intuition—those of space and time—and with twelve categories—among which "substance" and "cause"—that constitute the real sources of what we call "objectivity." The Copernican revolution to which Kant nailed his philosophical colors thus runs as follows: "Instead of asking what things are like in themselves, we should ask how they must be if they are to be known by us."[3]

It is still worth asking why Kant should have undertaken so heroic and dangerous a task and why he, a docile subject of the enlightened despot the King of Prussia, to whom he had once even dedicated a poem,[4] should have had to start a revolution. Unlike the causes that brought about the political revolutions of modern times, Kant's motives do not seem so very clear; yet, from a conceptual point of view, they turn out to be no less powerful and convincing.

Put simply, Kant too had no choice in the matter, given that philosophy as it was practiced at the time had reached a dead end, hanging

3

between a blind empiricism and an empty rationalism; so much so that one of Kant's most famous mottoes, "thoughts without content are empty, intuitions without concepts are blind,"[5] for all that it is (as we shall see in nauseating detail) highly debatable as a theoretical stance, offers a very exact portrait of the historical situation for which Kant sought to supply a cure. Thus, we may begin trying to see which forces were in action on the philosophical scene in the second half of the eighteenth century.

The rationalists and the Library of Babel

The rationalists, many of whom were German professors, looked back to the great reconciler that was Gottfried Wilhelm Leibniz (1646–1716). Suffice it to say that Leibniz dedicated himself to bringing harmony between Catholics and Protestants, to distracting Louis XIV from taking aim at Germany in favor of Egypt,[6] and even to bringing peace between the modern philosophy that began with Descartes (1596–1650) and the Scholasticism that drew inspiration from Aristotle. For this reason, rationalism can be identified in large part with the *Schulphilosophie* that brought medieval Scholasticism up to date with large doses of Cartesianism.

The rationalists' underlying idea was that we know through concepts. Knowing what an object is amounts to being able to list its features: soul is an unextended thing, body is an extended thing, a dog is a soulless domestic quadruped. In this spirit, the composition of a book of metaphysics is roughly the orderly formulation of definitions that are then combined in rational form so as to avoid contradictions. By the systematic aggregation of concepts, it becomes possible to realize the dream, first conceived in the Middle Ages by Raymond Lull (1232–1316) and then renewed in the Renaissance and in Descartes's time, of a "combinatorial art" that promised universal knowledge by means of the composition of concepts and, ultimately, of words.[7]

How was an art of this sort supposed to work? And, above all, did it work? Suppose we have to determine how many angels can dance on a pinhead. By definition, millions, given that, as we read in the dictionary, angels are pure spirits and have no body. Thus we have a ready answer: as many angels as you like can dance on a pinhead, just as there are infinitely many lines that pass through a point. If anyone objected that he had never seen an angel, the obvious answer would be that of course he hadn't because angels, being unextended, cannot be seen. This would not be a quip or a manner of speaking. Leibniz had elaborated a theory according to which the actual world, the one in which Julius Caesar crossed the Rubicon and John Lennon was shot by a fan, is just one possibility among very many that has been brought about, so that a complete metaphysics should concern itself with all the possibilities that do not contain a contradiction.[8]

Kant loathed this way of doing metaphysics. He was curious about the sciences and about travel, even though he himself never left Königsberg and its immediate environs, and he did not believe that dictionaries add anything to our knowledge. Moreover, he inherited a hatred for intellectualism from his professor of philosophy, Martin Knutzen (1713–1751), an early critic of hyper-rationalism. This is the source of his accusation against the Leibnizians that they did nothing but spin and weave purely nominal definitions in such a way that their metaphysical works were, at best, dictionaries and, at worst, fantasies born out of the combinations of words.

In his famous short story "The Library of Babel,"[9] Jorge-Luís Borges (1899–1986) illustrates the perverse brew that can come out of mixing the idea that the real is only one of the ways that possibility can manifest itself[10] with the dream of a combinatorial art doomed to speculate on the supposed advantages for knowledge gathering promised by the purely formal assemblage of the infinite resources of what is mere possibility. In that endless library, which contains all the combinations of the letters of the alphabet, there is, mixed in with all the infinite senseless books, everything, including the things we don't know (such as precisely what Caesar was thinking as he crossed the Rubicon and how many people there were in Rome that day), which is all to the good. But there is also the opposite of everything: a Caesar who does not cross the Rubicon, Rome defeated by Carthage, Caesar as Alexander the Great's grandfather, Hitler the philanthropist. Because we have no way of telling the true from the false, the library is useless; indeed, it would be better if it didn't exist, because most readers never had the luck to read a single passage that made full sense.[11]

Given that we are not stuck in the library of Babel, Kant—along with others who at the time began criticizing Leibniz[12]—could not draw inspiration from Borges. But the kernel of their dissatisfaction is this: how can we tell true from false unless we move from the world of mere possibility to that of actuality? And what is actuality unless it is primarily what we encounter in space and time or, as Hamlet had it, in heaven and earth? Kant observes[13] that there is a great difference between mathematics and metaphysics, a gap that the Leibnizians underestimated. Using the combination of symbols (Kant speaks of "construction," but the idea is the same[14]), I can reach fine results in mathematics. I can take a number at random, say 123, multiply it by another, 321, and get 39,483. The result is absolutely exact, and I'll get it every time I do the sum.

The trouble, nevertheless, is that mathematics is *not knowledge*,[15] because for Kant knowledge is formed from the encounter between concepts and the sensations that are produced by something that is physically real. Prior to that, one can *think*, which is a fine thing and can furnish some right answers, but it is different from knowing, as is easily demonstrated by considering the difference between thinking of a clock and looking at one in order to know what time it is. Thus, I have knowledge when I know, for instance, how many grains of wheat there are in a sack (say, 39,483), but not when I multiply 123 by 321. And the Leibnizians did not notice this difference because they were misled by the idea that there is no difference in kind between sensibility, which perceives things, and intellect, which thinks them, but only one of degree of clearness and distinctness.[16] Thus the supporters of rationalism behave like mathematicians when they do metaphysics insofar as they regard everything that is not contradictory as true.

From the point of view of concept-formation, there is nothing implausible about thinking, say, that Henri Bergson read the adventures of Flash Gordon (perhaps there would be a contradiction in his being a fan of Dylan Dog). Except that it isn't true or, more cautiously, we don't know that it is. And we can't build theories on the basis of such wild hypotheses, because mathematics seems clear and intuitive while the concepts are much less so, whether they refer to concrete objects[17] or to abstract notions—about which we may be completely in the dark. For instance, what exactly are we referring to when we speak about "freedom?" Kant rightly notes that most people, if not all, do not know exactly what they are saying when they use so vague a word.[18]

So as not to let metaphysics run unbridled, the maxim of prudence will then be not to compare one concept with another but, *insofar as it is possible* (and it is obviously not possible in all cases), to compare concepts with objects. If this is the cure, it would seem that it was the empiricists who had pointed to the right path to take, and Kant credits the leading empiricist of the day, David Hume (1711–1776), with having woken him from the "dogmatic slumbers"[19] into which he and a fair number of German professors had fallen.

The empiricists and Funes the Memorious

The basic idea of the empiricists was that all of our knowledge is derived from the senses: in the world, I encounter sensations and not concepts. Hence we can happily do without the purely conceptual organization of the universe that metaphysics offers. For instance we have the concept of "cause," but if we hadn't seen, say, a window that, as it opens, makes a vase fall, we would never have conceived of anything as a cause and we would not have included it in our dictionary. Likewise, we suppose that space has three dimensions: length, breadth and depth; but if we were subject to sensory deprivation, we might well not come up with the concepts of length and breadth. To say nothing of depth, which is not obvious even when we are endowed with senses and which calls for some supplementary experience: the man whom we now see as big because close was a dot on the horizon, and if we hadn't approached him it might not have occurred to us that, in addition to wide and high there is also the far and the near, that is, depth.

The moral that the empiricists drew was that, not just from the point of view of concept formation (as Kant would admit), but absolutely speaking; that our knowledge does not derive from concepts but rather from the sensible experience that is laid down by habit and reasoning. And concepts are just one quick, and often deceptive, way in which to codify that experience. Substance does not exist, but is the mere conjecture of a substrate that could exist without its accidents.[20] A cause is not a principle, but arises only from the fact that we often see one event follow another, and we think that the first determines the second.[21] The "I" is a mere bundle of sensations and not the unextended substance that Descartes thought it was.[22] At least one spatial dimension, depth, derives from experience.[23]

The empiricists, however, had trouble grasping that you can go some way without metaphysics, but not very far. And if we think of cause and substance, the self and space as mere upshots of our experiences, then philosophy, science, and morals are doomed to disappear, because the whole world crumbles in our hands. For a radical empiricist, everything is, in the long run, vain, and empiricism becomes the last stop before skepticism. After all, it is futile to inquire into the nature of things given that sooner or later they could change, and there is no deep difference between the laws of physics and the train timetable. These are the traditional and besetting problems of relativism, which does not necessarily need a justification of this sort.[24] The three biggest problems for the empiricists of the seventeenth and eighteenth centuries were certainty, the move from particular sensations to general ideas, and the relation between ideas and the things to which they referred.

The problem of *certainty* was the most alarming. Based on past experience, a turkey can conclude that every time the farmer comes, it will eat; but the day will come when the farmer will wring its neck. Given that, for the empiricist, all our knowledge, both of big things and small, is inductive, we are all in the position of the turkey: the law that makes the bulb light every time I switch the switch is limited by the fact that in the end the bulb will blow. Following this line, we ought even to doubt that the Sun will rise tomorrow (which will happen sooner or later). In this state of things, astronomy is a science that is uncertain, or at best a bit more credible than astrology. And this is a not entirely unwelcome conclusion, given that the empiricists developed this line of thought with a subtly antiscientific aim, seeking a residual space for philosophy. But nor is it terribly comforting.

From the practical point of view, the problem of *general ideas* was less pressing, but it generated serious theoretical difficulties. The empiricists could hardly deny that we have, in addition to the sensible impression of this dog, also the idea of a dog, which is applied to various instances of small dogs, big dogs, quiet dogs, barking dogs, dogs walking, and dogs at rest. But how do we get from the impressions to the idea? One suggestion is that we get there by a sort of mixture that makes perception more vague—Hume would say "enfeebles"—and that combines it with others: from one dog I take the snout, from another the tail, and so on.[25] In the nineteenth century there was at least one photographer who,[26] following up this idea, set out to find general ideas by superimposing many negatives so as to find the average criminal or the average member of the royal family. It is clear nevertheless that anything can come out of these dissolutions: for sure a dog, but also a bear or a hippopotamus, the average Victorian or Jack the Ripper. Moreover, if someone had a particularly good memory, like that of Ireneo Funes, hero of another Borges tale,[27] he would never form general ideas, but would have a distinct idea for each individual impression, not just for this leaf at 11:05 but also for the same leaf at 11:06; he could recall each instant of the previous day, but to do so would take a whole day, and so on.

Even without being Funes, the empiricists remain open to the attack, which has often and rightly been launched,[28] on the relation between ideas and things. In their view, we only ever have to do with

ideas, because individual sensations immediately become something fee-
bler and more general. Thus we are never in relation with, say, a brooch,
but only with the *idea* of a brooch. But what has the idea in common
with the brooch? For instance, and it is not negligible, the idea of a
brooch cannot prick you, just as you can't use the idea of a telephone
to make a call.

Having set out to be more down to earth than the rationalists, the
empiricists end up in danger of finding themselves with their hands full
of dust, or rather full of ideas of dust.

Refounding metaphysics by overturning the point of view

Against this rather depressing background, made all the more puzzling
by the greatness of the philosophers positioned on each side, the physicists, which is to say scientists who no longer recognized themselves
as philosophers, proceeded unabashed to dismantle the beliefs that had
held since antiquity and whose destruction undermined the standing of
metaphysics in the public eye. Here we find the detonator of Kant's
revolution. Many commentators have insisted, despite everything, on the
excessively formalist and hence rationalist nature of his outlook;[29] others have been keen to find in him a German approach to empiricism.[30]
Nevertheless, we have to deal with neither the one thing nor the other,
but rather with a rehabilitation of metaphysics by way of physics, of a
sort that neither the rationalists nor the empiricists had envisaged. We
may swiftly show how this is so.

A generation earlier than Kant, Voltaire (1694–1778) expressed a
commonsense satire of the learned metaphysicians, folk who believed
that they lived in the best of all possible worlds, that nothing was without its sufficient reason and that Chinese and Mexican were once the
same language. Folk, in short, who, like Don Ferrante in Manzoni's *The
Betrothed*, finding that the contagion is neither substance nor accident,
duly die of the plague cursing the stars like a hero in an opera by Metas-
tasio. Voltaire's satire came naturally because, in the meantime, Galileo
Galilei (1564–1642) and Isaac Newton (1642–1727) had set out the true
principles of a natural philosophy with a winning combination of conceptual hypotheses and empirical observations, bringing together what put
rationalism and empiricism asunder. Voltaire's conclusion, however, was
that metaphysics was more or less a form of soothsaying, a superstition
to be left behind.

Kant was much softer, not only on the world (as Hegel would reproach him) but also, and above all, on metaphysics. Indeed, he had compared what he called the "dreams of metaphysics" with the dreams of his contemporary spirit seer Emanuel Swedenborg (1688–1772) and concluded that concomitant illusions were in play.[31] And, as I noted earlier, Kant went so far as to credit Hume with having woken him from those dreams. But he did not believe, and for very strong reasons, that we can do without metaphysics. Many questions can be answered by experience: if I want to know the taste of grapefruit, all I have to do is try one. Others can be resolved by science, such as the cause of the tide or of allergies. Others cannot. Trivially, there is no single scientific experiment that can decide whether the collapse of the Twin Towers was one event or two;[32] or, what is more serious, whether we are free or not. The effects in each case are not themselves trivial, for if the collapse was a double event, the insurers must pay twice the amount, and if we are not free, then punishing and rewarding people will seem at the very least odd.

On the issue of freedom, as on those of the existence of the soul or of God, Kant does not arrive at a decision, or rather he says that we have to believe in them in order to make human life make sense. On the question of physical objects, on the other hand, his strategy involves taking up a different point of view. Where the naive onlooker sees the Sun set and concludes that it turns around the Earth, the expert (the post-Copernican physicist) knows that it is the Earth that rotates around the Sun. Whether he is a rationalist or an empiricist, the naive spectator looks at the world and believes he sees things as they are; the expert (the transcendental philosopher) knows that he is seeing things as they appear to us.

What advantage is there in being an expert? On the one hand, he doesn't pronounce as readily as the rationalists on matters that fall outside our experience; on the other, he is less evasive (and ultimately rudderless) than the empiricists about things we need to know. It seems obvious that we put something of ourselves into knowledge, insofar as it is up to the objects to conform themselves to us to some degree: we do not hear dog whistles and we do not see in infrared. Hence, we may allow a certain number of principles that are independent of experience and antecedent to it. As already hinted and as we shall see in more detail in the next chapter, there are basically five such principles: Self, Cause, Substance, Space, and Time. Contrary to what the rationalists thought, this does not mean that merely *thinking* something lets us know it. Content drawn from experience is needed. This is the meaning of the Copernican revolution,[33] a silent rebellion that is no more than an *overturning* of point of view, which Kant achieved in about 1770 at the relatively advanced age of forty-six.

The full elaboration of the critical philosophy would come even later with the *Critique of Pure Reason* (1781), the *Critique of Practical Reason* (1788), and the *Critique of Judgment* (1790). What exactly Kant was aiming to do no one has understood, and he probably didn't fully know himself. In particular, it is not clear whether he was meaning to reform metaphysics or bury it forever, and whether the three *Critiques* are freestanding treatises, as he sometimes asserts,[34] or mere introductory studies to a complete system that would be carried out at a later date either by Kant himself or by others.[35]

As the English philosopher J. L. Austin (1911–1960) once observed of Aristotle, in every great philosopher there are passages where he says it and passages where he takes it back,[36] and this is probably a consequence of the very queer proceeding that is philosophy. What is for sure is that in his lessons, Kant never discussed the critical philosophy, as expounded or introduced in the three *Critiques*, and that those books present themselves as aiming to answer three questions: What can I know?, What can I hope for?, and What ought I to do? (to which we might add, in the *Pragmatic Anthropology*, What is man?[37]).

This attempt was made by means of an examination of the three faculties that, for Kant, are fundamental to human beings: that of knowledge (*Critique of Pure Reason*); that of desire, namely, to do or not do something (*Critique of Practical Reason*); and that of pleasure and displeasure, or of the enjoyment or otherwise, as passive subjects, of an object or idea (*Critique of Judgment*). In each of these faculties we find, in various mixtures and combinations, each of the basic resources of human beings: sensibility, intellect, and reason, to which Kant sometimes adds imagination to form a bridge between sensibility and intellect. Roughly speaking, this is the grand subdivision of philosophical psychology handed down from Aristotle: sensibility receives external stimuli, imagination conserves them, intellect elaborates them, and reason (which corresponds to some degree to the active intellect of Aristotelian psychology) determines the ends of our behavior. It is above all reason that sets human beings apart insofar as it is the capacity to set ends for oneself, to respond to questions that vary from "What shall we do this evening?" to "What is it right for me to do?"; and Kant defines philosophy as the "teleology of human reason," by which he means the identification of ultimate ends. In line with this outlook, Kant was much preoccupied with the faculty of desire, that is, with the reply to how we should act in this life and whether it makes sense to expect rewards and punishments in another; this was why he also wrote a *Critique of Practical Reason*. The *Critique of Judgment*, on the other hand, has exercised a powerful but strange influence on the emergence of philosophical aesthetics in view of the fact that it is not a philosophy of art.[38] But by far the moxst influential of his works, not only because it was the first and made most fully explicit the Copernican revolution, remains the *Critique of Pure Reason*, which is my reason for giving it pride of place, or rather for focusing on the part of it that seems to me the most important, in this little book.

Given that our main subject is the Copernican revolution, my proposal is, in the next chapter, to isolate Kant's most fundamental claims and then, in Chapter 3, to show what he inherits from the tradition; in Chapter 4, to show what he invents; and, in Chapter 5, to show where he goes wrong. Chapters 6 through 8 set out the fundamental claims in detail, without comparing them directly with alternative theories, but taking literally Kant's idea that there are principles that hold good not just for science, but also for experience. Chapter 9 seeks to dismantle the sophisticated mechanism that stands behind the doctrines, while Chapter 10 presents Kant's evolution after the first *Critique*, and Chapter 11 aims at a reckoning with the revolution: its immediate effects and its legacy, its merits and its martyrs. Some of the chapters develop the main line of thought, while others integrate it with theoretical reflections and historical observations; to warn the reader in a hurry, these chapters bear the title annotation "Examination."

2

The basic claims

The scheme of the work

Let us begin by opening the *Critique of Pure Reason*. Because Kant presents the various topics of discussion in an order that is if not confusing at least hard to follow,[1] it may help to begin with a scheme of the work, in which the abbreviation "KrV" stands for "*Kritik der reinen Vernunft*," the book's German title.

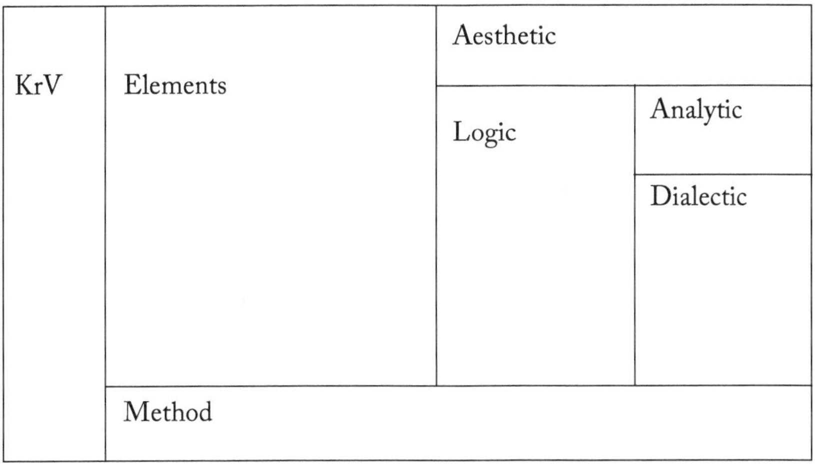

KrV	Elements	Aesthetic	
		Logic	Analytic
			Dialectic
	Method		

Figure 1. The scheme of the work

Thus, the book is divided into two sections that are very unequal in both size and complexity. On the one hand, the Elements describe the parts that make up our faculty for knowledge and, *at the same time*—a point to whose importance we shall return—the objects that can or cannot be known. The Elements are subdivided into the Aesthetic, which considers sensibility, from the Greek *aisthesis*, meaning sensation, and the

13

Logic, which considers intellect or *logos*. In its turn, the Logic breaks down into the Analytic, which concerns what we can know,[2] and the Dialectic, which concerns the matters that, not being objects of sensible awareness, we cannot know. On the other hand, there is the Method, which sets out the way we must proceed to organize our knowledge.

What, then, does the book discuss exactly, and what claims does it defend? At bottom, the idea is to discuss our lives, above all what we encounter in the external world when we open our eyes and take a walk in the street.

The metaphysics of experience

But what, exactly, do we find in the street? Not just cars and pedestrians but, for a transcendental philosopher, what we find are in the first place, *structures*: space, time, substances, and causes. Experience (and not the Self as Descartes believed, as did Kant a bit) is the thing to which we are closest, but it turns out to be very slippery. A mere listing of the things that happen to us is too scanty and of little interest, and an explanation of the deep structures, both within and without us, that underlie our experiences may be too much. What we have to do is find a balance, and it is not clear that Kant really succeeded in this, indeed, in my view, he tends too far in the direction of *explanation* rather than *description*. How so?

In a well-known study,[3] the English philosopher P. F. Strawson (1919–2006) argues that the *Critique of Pure Reason* isolates the minimum requirements for having an experience and sets out the main features of the central core of even the least sophisticated human thought that makes up the underlying node of our relation with the world. It is precisely a metaphysics of experience that is concentrated in the Analytic. Strawson summarizes it in six theses, which he regards as strict and acceptable, maintaining that they are set to oppose an implausible transcendent idealism of the sort dealt with in the Dialectic. Here are the theses of what Strawson regards as a good metaphysics:

1. that experience essentially exhibits temporal succession;

2. that experience refers to a necessary unity of consciousness;

3. that it applies to objects distinguishable from the experience that we have of them;

4. that those objects are essentially spatial;

5. that they enter into a single coherent spatio-temporal framework; and

6. that certain principles of permanence and causality must be satisfied.

Is this really a metaphysics of experience? That remains to be seen.

In the first place, Strawson's rejigging seeks to set aside the more extreme sides of Kant's theory. This is an entirely reasonable choice if the aim is to set out the minimally acceptable content of the transcendental philosophy. But it runs the risk of obscuring some implications that Kant himself took to be central, for all that they border on what we have seen Strawson describing, with well-grounded disapproval, as a "transcendent metaphysics." But this is not the main problem.

Even with his reasonable pruning, Strawson wants Kant to be a descriptive metaphysician, a sort of phenomenologist of ordinary experience of the kind we return to in Chapter 3. In this way, he expels the transcendent metaphysician who does speak about God, the soul, and the world at the same time he suppresses the large amount of science that Kant deploys to explain rather than describe experience.

Strawson's approach is misleading because the transcendent metaphysician does seem to be reasonable in treating God, the soul, and the world not as objects but as ideas. And where he does so, the Kant who is a theoretician of experience is almost never a descriptive metaphysician but a prescriptive one, in a way that, once more, we expand on in the next chapter. And even there, he has precisely confused science with experience and takes himself to be discussing the latter while he is in fact offering a scientific vision of the world.

If we are aiming at a less indulgent reconstruction of Kant's philosophy, it does not help to smooth away the thorninesses; in the case in hand, in place of Strawson's six theses, we may substitute some others that are rather stronger, five of them ontological (concerning what there is) and two epistemological (concerning what we know about what there is), which form the basic structure of my exposition.

If I can show that the *Critique of Pure Reason* really can be summed up in these theses, I shall also have vindicated my overall position, namely that Kant's view seems to offer a theory of experience but really presents a theory of science, precisely because it confuses the two levels. This might seem a trifling and unappealing conclusion, but in my view it has the

advantage of setting out economically the core of Kant's thought, the
causes of its success, and the reasons for its relative obsolescence after
two hundred years.

Five ontological theses

Granted this premise, here are the five ontological theses:

1. Thesis about **Space**. "By means of outer sense, a property of
   our mind, we represent to ourselves objects as outside us, and
   all without exception as in space."[4] In other words, there is a
   container, space, with three dimensions, that contains all the
   extended things, from atoms and molecules upward, and that
   precedes them.

2. Thesis about **Time**. "Neither coexistence nor succession would
   ever come within our perception, if the representation of time
   were not [. . .] *a priori*."[5] There is another container, time,
   that contains everything contained in the spatial container,
   plus other, more fleeting objects (such as memories and
   expectations), existing in time but not in space and possessing
   duration but not extension.

3. Thesis about **Substance**. "In all change of appearances
   substance is permanent."[6] We do not learn of this unvarying
   substance from habit, but we are endowed with a concept
   that precedes experience and that helps us understand, for
   instance, that water, ice, and steam are three states of a single
   substance. Without the concept, we would not get there.

4. Thesis about **Cause**. "All alterations take place in conformity
   with the law of the connection of cause and effect."[7] Here,
   too, if we did not know, prior to any experience, that fire
   makes water boil, the senses alone would be unable to teach
   us that it does.

5. Thesis about the **Self**. "It must be possible for the "I think" to
   accompany all my representations."[8] There is an unextended
   and unchanging point, not unlike the Cartesian *cogito*, but a
   little more elaborate inasmuch as it contains not only doubts
   but also the four foregoing points of space, time, substance,

and cause. Every time I have a sensation or a thought, the self registers it and refers it to itself (*I* am hot; *I* see red; *I* am thinking of Pegasus or Napoleon). If it did not do so, the experiences and thoughts would attach to nothing, as is the case when we perform some action, such as shutting the door, without thinking about it, and then we can't remember doing it.

Each of these theses has its own target: the theses about space and about time are responses to Leibniz and to George Berkeley (1685–1753), who regarded space and time as results of the relations among objects and not as a priori forms; that about substance aims to correct John Locke (1632–1704), who held substance to be a mental construct generated by habit; those about cause and about the self have, as we have already noted, Hume as their target.

Two epistemological theses

Mediated by the thesis about the self, which is both a knowing subject and a known object, the ontological theses rest upon two epistemological theses.

1. The thesis of **Conceptual Schemes**. "Thoughts without content are empty, intuitions without concepts are blind."[9] Kant was the first philosopher to maintain that, in order to have experiences, it is necessary to have conceptual schemes (transcendental idealism); and he was probably the first—at least among philosophers—to maintain that only what is in space and time exists (empirical realism).[10] The crucial point about the thesis of conceptual schemes, which sums up and makes possible the five ontological theses, is that it is not enough to be able to see to have eyes: we need spectacles to turn unfocused and disorderly perception into clear and coherent experiences. These spectacles are the concepts that are articulated into judgments from which the categories follow.

2. This thesis is connected to another, that of the **Phenomenon**, which encapsulates the meaning of the Copernican revolution:

"The undetermined object of an empirical intuition is entitled *phenomenon*."[11] We do not have direct traffic with things in themselves, but only with objects that appear to us through the mediation of space and time (the pure forms of the intuition and the perceptual apparatus that carries them), of the self and of the conceptual schemes or categories. Nevertheless, the phenomena are not mere appearances, but rather exist no less than the self does, which is itself known only as a phenomenon.[12]

Where to find them

Filling in the table drawn at the beginning of this chapter, what follow are the places in which the substantive claims are to be found in the *Critique of Pure Reason*:

KrV	Elements	**Aesthetic** Space Time	
		Logic I think	**Analytic** Substance Cause
			Dialectic
	Method		

Figure 2. Aesthetics, Logic, and Analytics

Before proceeding, however, it is useful to take account of Kant's debts to earlier tradition, the novelties he introduces, and the underlying fallacy he commits in confusing science and experience. These are the topics of the next three chapters; the reader who is in a hurry and wishes to cut to the chase may skip directly to Chapter 6.

3

What is inherited
(Examination)

New wine in old bottles

What did Kant owe to the tradition that preceded him? To show what he inherited, I shall try to reply to four questions:

1. Is there a metaphysics in Kant, and if so, what is it like?

2. What were the models for the *Critique of Pure Reason*?

3. What was Kant's winning move?

4. What are its consequences?

Kant's metaphysics

His contemporaries regarded Kant as the "Prussian Hume," and he has gone down in history as the destroyer of metaphysics, especially if that is understood rather widely as "transcendence."[1] But if that were really so, how can we explain the fact that he gave lessons in metaphysics for fully thirty years, at just the time he was thinking through and bringing to press the three *Critiques*? And this is a teaching activity about which we have plenty of evidence: the Berlin Academy of Sciences in its edition of his works reproduces what his students collected of his lectures on metaphysics, which were essentially a commentary on the *Metaphysica* of the Leibnizian Alexander Gottlieb Baumgarten (1714–1762).[2] So, what was the discipline that he explained in lessons?

It was the oldest and most venerable of the branches of philosophy. In the fourth century B.C., Aristotle (384–322 B.C.) had excogitated in some of his writings a "first philosophy" that brings together the most general principles, which are shared by the sciences and by common sense and which can be used to classify the whole of reality and, so to speak, to draw up an orderly catalogue of the world. The writings that deal with these principles were collected, along with Aristotle's other lecture materials, by Andronicus of Rhodes in the first century B.C. Andronicus was a philologist who, for the sake of convenience, dubbed these writings "metaphysics" because he classified them as the books that came after the books of physics (*meta ta physika biblia*). At the beginning of the seventeenth century,[3] the most general part of the universal catalogue sketched by Aristotle and developed by the scholastics, the theory of the object, came to be known as "ontology," or the doctrine of being in general.

As we shall shortly see, ontology includes everything that is in heaven and earth, the realm of the objects that are available to experience, while metaphysics deals with what goes beyond or transcends it.[4] These two topics are the main matter of the *Critique of Pure Reason*.

Nevertheless, there is nothing obvious about the claim that a critique of reason constitutes an ontology. And this is so for at least three reasons, two of which derive from Kant himself and one from his commentators. First, Kant regarded metaphysics as a groping in the dark after what are, in any case, simple concepts,[5] and he thought that the metaphysics of his own day amounted to nothing more than "castles in Spain."[6] In the second place, he maintained that "ontology" is too puffed up a word, that it should be replaced by an analysis and a critique of reason.[7] And, third, the consideration that derives from his interpreters, the transcendental philosophy is presented even in high school as something quite different and new, something that has nothing in common with the medieval, scholastic, or modern tradition.

Does it, then, make sense to speak of Kant's "metaphysics" or "ontology"? In spite of everything, indeed it does, if for no other reason than because it would otherwise be even less clear what it was he looking for. As we have seen, his distaste for the metaphysics of his own time is certain, but it does not tell us much. Yet it is not hard to see how the *Critique of Pure Reason* inherits the system and the vocabulary of the Leibnizians (and hence, through them those of the Scholastics), bringing them together with the various empiricist essays, treatises and enquiries into human nature. To illustrate how this is so, we would do well to look again at our scheme of the first *Critique*.

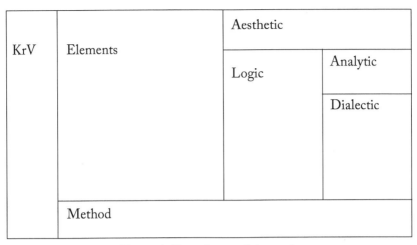

KrV	Elements	Aesthetic	
		Logic	Analytic
			Dialectic
	Method		

Figure 1. The scheme of the work

Now, as regards the continuity between metaphysics and ontology, the structure that Kant builds into the doctrine of the Elements (i.e., what this table shows as the bulk of the *Critique*) reflects the traditional subdivisions of metaphysics[8] as set out at the end of the sixteenth century by the Spanish Jesuit Francisco Suárez (1548–1617)[9] and taken up in the eighteenth by the Leibnizian Christian Wolff (1679–1754).[10] The Analytic corresponds to general metaphysics, or ontology, which Kant defined in his lectures as the doctrine that "contains all the pure concepts that we have of things *a priori*."[11] On the other hand, the Dialectic belongs to special metaphysics, which is the rational treatment, prior to any experience, of those peculiar objects, which for Kant turn out to be ideas, which are the soul, the world, and God.

Thus, the reader of the Analytic has before him Kant's ontology, a work of construction and not of destruction. And it is not by chance that two influential but otherwise opposed readings of Kant, that of Strawson and that of Martin Heidegger (1889–1976),[12] have concentrated on this first part, and I follow suit. For it is here that Kant brings together what we have already heard Strawson calling a "metaphysics of experience" and that Heidegger calls an "analysis of finite human being," which amounts to the same thing, said with more passion. On the other hand, the Dialectic corresponds to what Strawson calls "transcendent metaphysics"; it is ground not to be entered on lightly lest we end up talking about things that are, literally, not in heaven or on earth. Its rightful realm is that of morality, and we find its most coherent development in the *Critique of Practical Reason*, and for that reason, we discuss it briefly in Chapter 10.

If this account of how things stand is plausible, which I hope it is, then Kant's ontology, understood as general metaphysics, is to be found in the parts of the table that are colored gray. Those in light gray are mixed treatment of both general and special metaphysics.

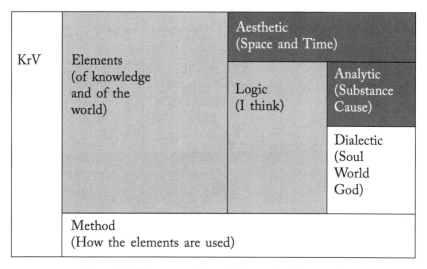

Figure 3. Elements of knowledge and of the world

We thus come to the third problem, which, as I have said, is due in large part to the commentators. In a move that was much in vogue with nineteenth-century neo-Kantians and that has since become a commonplace in handbooks of the history of philosophy, the *Critique of Pure Reason* is presented as destroying metaphysics on the following grounds. Insofar as Kant moves the focus from the object to the subject, he makes a clean break with the preceding tradition and sets on foot the conception of philosophy as theory of knowledge rather than as theory of the object. The strongest evidence for this transformation would lie in Kant's own description of his philosophy as "transcendental," that is, as concerned with the a priori conditions of knowledge, and not, as in the old metaphysics, with those of the objects known.

Nevertheless, this very point, which is supposed to mark the watershed between the old and the new itself, masks an underlying continuity. Perhaps for us, the word "transcendental" seems like a Kantian term of art, a neologism that is now a bit long in the tooth, dating as it does to the eighteenth century. But in point of fact, the tooth is a fossil: the medieval Schoolmen, building on Boethius (ca. 480—526), already had their transcendental or, rather, their transcendentals.[13] In their account of logic, the transcendentals are the features of objects that are so general as to be broader in scope than the categories themselves, because they apply to *all* objects whatsoever. Unlike the categories, they do not classify anything whatsoever because they list the properties of any being *whatsoever.* Saying that birds fly does not distinguish sparrows from tits, but saying that every being is one (the one that it is and not another), true (precisely itself), and good (fair enough: they were thinking in terms of createdness) can be applied to anything at all, from the watch on my wrist to Pegasus. This they held for the perfectly respectable reason that everything is something; otherwise it is not a thing. And "to be something"[14] means precisely satisfying the minimum requirements of the transcendentals.

In line with his own revolution, Kant rewrites everything from the viewpoint of the knowing subject. That is, he does not look for his transcendentals in the world but in the mind. And this does not get in the way of his saying in his university lectures that "the highest concept in all of human knowledge is the concept of the object in general,"[15] which is exactly what St. Thomas Aquinas (1221–1274) had said about the being (*ens*) of a thing (*res*).

Below the transcendentals, we come to the categories, which are the less elevated or slippery kinds that can, therefore, be put to some sort of use. Aristotle,[16] and, in his wake, the Schoolmen, picked out ten of these. This was two fewer than Kant would, by other means, arrive at, listing four families each composed of three categories, which he held to constitute the range of relations that the mind enters into with the world when it formulates a judgment.[17] These are *quantity* (everything is big or small, long or short); *quality* (everything is hot or cold, loud or soft, etc.); *relation* (we encounter substances, or causes, or objects and events that do not interact with each other); and *modality* (each thing is merely possible, or it is actual, or it may even be necessary).

Relative to the classical approach, with its emphasis on the object, Kant appears a rather circumspect revolutionary who goes looking for his categories in the mind, in the judgments of the intellect, rather than in the world or in objects. In Kant's view, this was called for because, if we start with the world rather than with the mind, we end up with a disorderly and "rhapsodic" catalogue of the sort that Aristotle produced. What we have, then, is doubtless a transformation of ontology rather than a break with the past.

The models of the *Critique of Pure Reason*

Granting, then, the close relationship between the critique of reason and ontology, that is, between Kant and metaphysics, let us proceed to his relations with the moderns.[18] If we follow through what we have been saying until now, we can identify by name the authors of those bits of the *Critique* that remain invariant in their rather strangely renamed new homes:

Locke, *Essay Concerning Human Understanding,* 1689	Clauberg, *Elements of Philosophy or Ontosophy,* 1647	Baumgarten, *Aesthetics,* 1750	
		Suárez *Metaphysical Disputations,* 1597	Wolff, *Ontology,* 1730
			Descartes, *Metaphysical Meditations,* 1641
	Descartes, *Discourse on the Method,* 1637 Lambert, *New Organon,* 1764		

Figure 4. The scheme of inspirations

Proceeding to the details:

1. In calling the part that deals with sensibility "aesthetic," Kant is following Baumgarten, who used the name for the science of sensible knowledge.[19]

2. The idea of a critique of reason derives from the subjective viewpoint adopted by Descartes and then developed by way of empirical psychology by Locke.

3. Collecting the ontological investigation under the title of "elements" is reminiscent of the ancient usage of Euclid (third century B.C.) and revived, for instance, by the German Cartesian Johannes Clauberg (1622–1665) who was the first to use "ontology" (or rather "*Ontosophy*") in a book title;[20] the various doctrines of the elements that were composed from the seventeenth century down to the time of Kant all amount, whether implicitly or explicitly, to ontologies, that is, they form reasoned catalogues of the things that are.

4. As we have seen, the distinction between the Analytic and the Dialectic reflects the Suárez-Wolff distinction between general metaphysics ("ontology") and special metaphysics and represents a mediation between Scholasticism and the new, subjectivist metaphysics that Descartes founded.

5. The transcendental doctrine of the method is a kind of *Discourse on the Method*;[21] indeed we can see in the distinction between the Elements and the Method in the *Critique* a reversal of the Cartesian order insofar as for Kant the exposition of the method follows rather than introduces the ontological analysis.

6. Finally, the systematic nature of the method of pure reason and the fact that it calls for an "architectonic" is due not just to the suggestion of Baumgarten but also to Kant's friend and correspondent, the Alsatian mathematician Johann Heinrich Lambert (1728–1777).

From our point of view, these names serve more as reference points than as sources for Kant: he was not much interested in the history of philosophy and did not go much beyond synopses[22] and manuals;[23] he probably never read Suárez and may never even have heard of Clauberg. So much for the names; let us now consider the things, namely, once more the conflict between empiricism and rationalism.

We just mentioned the word "architectonic," which is a slightly baroque term in need of some explanation. The fundamental assumption of Kant's distribution of the questions he faces is that knowledge turns out to be "architectonic," that is to say, capable of turning a mere aggregate of knowledge into a system.[24] Kant is very insistent on this substantive point, which in turn corresponds to the idea that experience, too, is systematic. The parallelism here leads him to impose an immediate conceptual scheme on spatio-temporal experiences: certain knowledge is just that which we have a priori, that is, independent of experience but without transcending experience, lest we end up like Swedenborg, claiming to communicate directly from London with spirits in Sumatra. Kant's innovation relative to the contemporary rationalism consists in taking a light dose of empiricism and a heavy dose of mathematical physics, which in his view make up a plausible and winning metaphysics able to refer to objects in space and time.

There are two important consequences of the clearly empiricist-inspired critique of metaphysics and its claims. One is the idea of combining the traditional ontological enquiry into objects in general with a psychological investigation of the human intellect. At one remove, this is to be found in Locke,[25] but it appears in Kant through the mediation of Wolff and Baumgarten, who had adopted it into their metaphysics moderating Leibniz's hyper-rationalism. The other, deriving from Hume,[26] is the idea that, at one and the same time, experience is the basis for all knowledge, thus putting rationalism out of the picture, yet inadequate insofar as empirical knowledge is always and only inductive and hence merely probable. This fact suggested to Kant that, despite the wild appearances, the rationalists were not entirely wrong to pursue their line.

The Copernican revolution can thus be seen as arising out of the conflict between two factors. On the one hand, there is the idea that a critique of reason as the knowing faculty has to be conducted along the lines of empiricist psychology and philosophical anthropology. On the other, there is the fact that, in Kant's view, the treatises in question proposed a merely empirical psychology and, as such, were unable to explain the genesis of our knowledge or, rather, tended to view even our most abstract knowledge as the upshot of simple perceptions.

With this move, Kant hopes to defuse both the skeptical potential of empiricism and the vacuousness of rationalism. Instead of investigating how things are in themselves, we concentrate on how, under the guise of a necessary appearance, they present themselves to us. But this "we" or, rather, this "I" is not an individual psyche, but an a priori structure that holds for everyone and that determines once and for all our relation with the world.

Kant's second great theoretical maneuver is thus based on a further conflict. This time between, on the one hand, the idea that only experience can give us genuinely ampliative knowledge, what Kant would call synthetic rather than analytic;[27] and, on the other, the fact that empirical acquaintance is insufficient because it is merely probable. And the resolution lies in the idea that the task of "first philosophy" is not to find a bunch of incontrovertible facts that ensure us a fulcrum with which not to lift the world, as Archimedes wanted, but to stop the world from wobbling under the attacks of skepticism.

Putting together these two moves, we have Kant's fundamental theory, in which empiricism provides the reference to psychology and experience, and rationalism brings along ontology and the a priori.

The naturalization of physics

The overturning thus involves not objects but the point of view from which they are looked at. This is the crucial third point to be made in this chapter and for Kant's theory.

Every reader of the *Critique of Pure Reason* asks himself an obvious question: What is it that Kant is describing? Is it the human mind or, rather, the necessary and pure structures of the minds of humans and perhaps other beings suitably similar to them? Or is it the world, given that Kant talks about substance, cause, space, and time? The answer is that, like the one-to-one scale map imagined by Lewis Carroll,[28] Kant is describing both things at once, because, in virtue of the Copernican revolution, mind and world are two sides of the same coin.[29] Put simply, this is the reason why it is natural for Kant to make his theory of objects overlap with his theory of knowledge and his theory of the world overlap with his theory of the mind that knows it. Now we have to explore what makes for such an identification. How could Kant reply to the obvious objection that what we have here is psychology? How could he not have taken account of the fact that, if this is how things are, then the study of astronomy and of chemistry is, at the end of the day, the very same thing as the study of consciousness? He does so simply by asserting that the laws that the mind gives to the world are those of physics. Let us now try to clarify this point.

As we hinted in Chapter 1, when Kant began his career, there were two theses that were broadly accepted in certain philosophical circles, especially those critical of Leibniz and Wolff, where he himself was educated. The first was that ampliative knowledge can only arise from sensible experience. This was far from being obvious, given that even as late as the eighteenth century, logics were being composed that had the ambition of advancing knowledge, reviving the tradition of logic as a sort of art of discovery (*ars inveniendi*[30]). The second thesis was that,

despite or rather because of its informative wealth, experience could not
guarantee the same level of necessary certainty that was assured by logic
and mathematics.

As a matter of historiography, the great neo-Kantian Ernst Cassirer
(1874–1945)[31] described in great detail this movement for the revision
of rationalism in France and Germany in the eighteenth century. But
to understand the theoretical force of Kant's move, we may consider
the decisive argument that ran more or less as follows.[32] The traditional
answer given to the empiricists, who believed that all our knowledge
comes from experience and cannot be more than probable, was to point to
mathematics, which could hardly be regarded as merely "more probable"
than the hypothesis that a red sky at night means good weather. This
was the rationalists' move. Yet Kant shies away from the purely rational,
that is to say nominal, constructs of their metaphysics. For these turn
out to be made up of nothing but analytic propositions, like dictionary
entries. Mathematics, nevertheless, offers synthetic propositions, which
say more than their definitions: after all, a computer is more inventive
than a dictionary. But they do not amount to knowledge because, in
Kant's view, we have knowledge only of things in space and time, and
this is not true of numbers.

Here, then, is the solution. *Mathematical physics* is the true way to
get to notions that are both as secure as mathematical operations yet as
thick or contentful as those we draw from experience. The consequence is
that, through the Copernican revolution, the task of metaphysics becomes
that of the naturalization of physics by showing that *the way in which
science is done is the same as that in which experience is had.* This move
opens the path that would be taken by the overwhelming majority of
philosophers in the nineteenth and twentieth centuries[33] but that would
also lead to a fatal misunderstanding.

Which? Unlike Galileo, Kant did not think that nature could be
a book written in the language of mathematics, open to be read by a
scientist who investigates it with the appropriate tools. Rather, he held
that our experience is in every way the same as the knowledge with
which physics provides us. This is because both rely on exactly the same
principles, which Kant sums up in the "system of the principles of pure
intellect." Given that he chose to name his revolution after the man who,
at least in the modern understanding, taught that the Sun never really
sets, Kant was, by doing so, also choosing as the privileged viewpoint not
what we see (for instance, we could never see the Sun *falling* between
the mountains, because its movement seems too slow) but what we know
about the relative motions.

As we have seen, the appeal to physics and to experience, and, at a deeper level, to physics *as* experience, is severely hampered by the variability of what our senses *encounter* in the world—as opposed to what they *know* of it[34]—which makes it all the harder to build up a metaphysics of experience. As for both the empiricists and the rationalists, so also for Kant, necessity turns out to be a purely logical notion insofar as talk of "material necessity"[35] involves much the same sort of contradiction we find in a "roundsquare." To restore necessity to what is, Kant has to show that some of its most general features are necessary. As it is set out in the preface to the second edition of the *Critique of Pure Reason*, the argument proceeds in four basic phases as follows:[36]

1. **Logic** is a certain and perfect doctrine that concerns thought rather than the world and hence cannot be a source of knowledge;

2. Since ancient times **Mathematics** has shown itself able to do without experience.[37] Kant's idea is that when the first geometers studied the properties of triangles, they were aware that they were not *copying* triangles or *describing* the properties of triangular objects in the way that a botanist classifies the properties of a plant; rather, they were *constructing* shapes on the basis of primitive concepts and making use of intuitions. Nevertheless, not even mathematics furnishes knowledge, but only thought.

3. With the Copernican revolution, modern **Physics** has shown itself to be in a position not merely to complete the discoveries of the Greek mathematicians but also to interrogate nature, not from the position of the learner but from that of the judge. That is to say, the modern physicist can organize experience within the a priori scheme of mathematical laws. In this way, we shall have propositions that have the certainty of mathematics but that are also as cognitively thick as those derived from the senses.

4. The task left over for any **Metaphysics** that aspires to be a science is that of naturalizing physics. In this, the aim is to show that it is not just one way of knowing reality, of "interpreting nature,"[38] but rather that physics represents the way our senses are set up and our intellect functions. This is the task performed in the Analytic. The aim of the Dialectic

is to sweep away the knowledge-claims of all propositions
that lack a verifiable empirical content and to reallocate the
drives that throw up these propositions to another realm,
namely that of morals.

Consequences

The aim of this is to achieve the squaring of the circle. Sensible experience, which is real, can be appealed to with the certainty that is under-
written by the mathematized science of nature, whose successes Kant
presents as incontrovertible and which he recommends without further
ado in metaphysical terms. *The price of this is that Kant's metaphysical
principles are derived from physics.*[39]

This is the crucial move that, in Chapter 5, I develop under the
label "transcendental fallacy." Dazzled by the successes of physics, Kant
muddled science with experience, epistemology with ontology. Epistemology has to do with what we know and how we know it, such as the
computer that is in front of my eyes; ontology has to do with what is
independently of whether or not I know anything about it, such as the
computer on your desk.[40]

Of course, it is easy to confuse epistemology and ontology. Yet,
in doing so, Kant not only made a very common mistake, but, by not
restricting himself to pointing out the structures of our ordinary experience, he also committed himself to what has come to be known as
"prescriptive" or "corrective" metaphysics.[41] What he ends up doing, or
wanting to do, is quite another thing. He corrects common sense and
translates experience in the light of what happens to be our best scientific
theory. In a corrective metaphysics, we must do away with expressions
like "the sun has gone down" (that is not, after all, what has happened),
"the coffee has cooled down" (we should rather say that its has transferred
kinetic energy to the environment) or "I have burned myself" (instead,
we say something about C fibers firing).

Now, there's nothing amiss about proposing a corrective metaphysics, and it would be hard to imagine a purely descriptive metaphysics,
given that the two levels are in continuous symbiosis, at least for an
adult of today. But Kant, and most of the philosophers who followed
him down that primrose path, made it a point of system and principle
to confuse the two levels and the two attitudes they carry with them.[42]
It is neither the first nor the last time that the road to damnation is

paved with good intentions, but for Kant and for us, the determination to follow it has been enormous. Before setting out the fallacy involved, I would nevertheless like to bring to light Kant's main innovations.

4

What is novel
(Examination)

Kant and the platypus

To fix Kant in his times, in the last chapter we played the game of "new wine in old bottles," which in philosophy is often enough old wine in new bottles, or, to drop the figure, we tried to show how much he owed to his predecessors.

The moment has now come to render unto Kant that which is Kant's and to see, along with the continuities, the groundbreaking novelties, which are in large part connected to the substantive theses set out in Chapter 2. Let us first of all look at our standard table:

KrV	Elements Synthetic a priori judgments	**Aesthetic** Space Time Phenomena	
		Logic "I think" Conceptual schemes	**Analytic** Judgments Categories Deduction Schematism Principles
			Dialectic Antinomies
	Method How the elements are used		

Figure 5. The scheme of innovations

The novelties of the *Critique of Pure Reason* can be identified on at least four levels: (1) theory of knowledge, (2) theory of mind, (3) ontology, and (4) theory of reasoning or logic. It is not difficult, then, to understand why the composition of the book took ten years, not to mention all the earlier philosophical experience it is freighted with. As sometimes happens, new things are referred to with new, or renewed, words. Let us list them in the order we have already indicated.

1. **Phenomenon** and **Noumenon**. This pair of terms is the great transformation in the *theory of knowledge*. What they correspond to in the claim made by the Copernican revolution is the thesis that we never know things in themselves, but only as they appear to us through the filter of the two pure forms of intuition and of the twelve categories.

2. **Deduction, Schematism, Imagination**. These are the keywords of Kant's *theory of mind*. As we shall see, they explain how thought can regulate experience.

3. **One hundred thalers**. This is Kant's watchword in *ontology*. Against the rationalist tradition, Kant held that existence is not a logical determination or predicate, but an ontological presupposition. The table in front of me is not made of wood, with a lamp and a computer as well as being *existent*; rather it *is*, and the way that it is is to be made of wood, with a lamp and a computer, and so forth.

4. **Synthetic a priori judgments**. This is Kant's real innovation in the *theory of reasoning*. Kant proposes a new logic that is applicable not just to thought but also to experience. In place of analytic judgments based on the Principle of Non-contradiction he puts those of the synthetic a priori, which are guided by the rule that every experience must refer back to the synthetic unity of apperception, which is nothing other than the "I think."

It would be unfair to underestimate Kant's innovations, or at least his genius for recycling. In treatises of pre-Kantian philosophy, we find very little of these notions, and even when there are hints of them in writers close to Kant, we generally have to do with very different contents. The "transcendental logic" is an absolute novelty. The name "phenomenology" was coined by Lambert,[1] but he meant by it a method for correcting illusions, that is to say, in a sense opposite to the one Kant uses in the contrast between phenomenon and noumenon. The psychologist Johannes Nicolaus Tetens (1736–1807) had discussed imagination in a book that Kant had read while he was working on the *Critique*,[2] but he did not give it the decisive and highly influential role that it would occupy in the reelaboration worked through by Kant and his followers. Neither the empiricists nor the Leibnizians showed any inkling either of the Deduction or of the Schematism, given that, from their different sides, both narrowed the distance between sensibility and intellect and, hence, had no call for a mediation.[3] The fallacies of the ontological arguments that treat existence as a predicate were recognized in the Middle Ages but had been forgotten with the return of rationalism in Descartes, who had rehabilitated the argument, and in Leibniz, who thought of existence as just one mode that can be added to the essence or logical definition.[4]

Before proceeding to the analysis, there is a further point to be made. The first two groups of Kant's innovations—in the theory of knowledge and the theory of mind—presuppose a strong idealism, while the other two—in ontology and in logic—are strongly realist. Thus, Kant's whole edifice is built on sand, and this ambiguity may explain why it has been given so many different readings over the years.

Phenomenon and noumenon

At the core of his theory of knowledge, Kant introduces the distinction between the phenomena, which are how things appear—not as misleading or false perceptions, but as the necessary appearances—and the noumena, which are how things are in themselves and to which, ex hypothesi, we have no access. We come back to this in detail in Chapter 6, so we may be brief here. But we have here an important novelty, so much so that Arthur Schopenhauer (1788–1860)[5] regarded Kant's theory as a development of the intuitions of Plato and Indian philosophy. Yet for Kant, the thesis that everything is appearance bears no trace of mysticism: the phenomena do not point toward a thing-in-itself that is inaccessible to the unenlightened; rather, it is the only knowledge available both to common sense and to philosophy within a scientific worldview.

Deduction, schematism, and imagination

In his *theory of mind*, Kant seeks mediating structures that will facilitate communication between the level of concepts and that of perception. And he has to build a speculative or "transcendental"[6] psychology with his bare hands to respond to this need, thus producing strange conceptual platypuses whose origins are to be found in the tension built up in Kant by, on the one hand, the sharp separation of a sort alien to Leibniz and the empiricists between sensibility and intellect, and, on the other, the impossibility of sensible experience without concepts.

The three most challenging of these platypuses are (a) the Deduction, which shows that the mind's categories make the world possible; (b) the Schematism, which explains how the pure concepts of the intellect apply to experience; and (c) the transcendental Imagination, which is an amphibious faculty, part sensible, part intelligible, and also creative. This third platypus is given an essential role to play both in the Deduction and in the Schematism at the crucial moment in which a bridge has to be built between mind and world. These are matters on which I have much to say in Chapters 9 and 10.

The hundred thalers

As regards the realist innovations in ontology, Kant specifies the focal meaning of "to be" as "to be real" or "to exist in space and time." For all its seeming obviousness, this specification has a corollary of primary importance. Namely that, contrary to what many philosophers had held prior to Kant, "being" is not a predicate or an attribute of an object, on a par with "red," "swift," or "smelly." Rather, it is the condition for something's really being red, swift, or smelly. In the famous example that Kant offers, a hundred real thalers are identical, as regards their concept—when merely thought—to a hundred ideal thalers. But the conceptual identity does not hide what Hemingway would have described as the difference between to have and to have not, which in ontology Hamlet would have expressed as the difference between to be or not to be.

Now, the idea that the primary meaning of "to be" is "to be in space and time" is the conception that underlies the selection of physics as the science to which metaphysics refers. It is also the upshot of Kant's negotiations with both empiricism and rationalism. Specifically, in the light of what he calls the failure of the "transcendental topic," he accuses the Leibnizians of treating sensations as confused concepts and concepts as clear and distinct sensations. Just as Leibniz intellectualizes phenomena, Locke sensibilizes concepts.[7] What both miss is the not negligible fact that whereas sensations come to us passively through the eyes, ears, nose, tongue, and skin, thoughts are generated actively by the brain, that is, typically behind the eyes, between the ears, and under the hair. These are two channels that are absolutely distinct, physically, logically, and metaphysically. If we do not take account of this fact, we lose the difference between money that is merely thought and money that is actually present, and we cannot afford to be so remiss.

This is where the famous hundred thalers come in. As the Kantian Friedrich Albert Lange (1828–1875)[8] explained, a treasury bond whose face (ideal) value was one hundred thalers was convertible, four years after Kant's death, for twenty-five (real) thalers. The difference is clear enough, and it is evident why Kant chose the example, which goes to the heart of the question. The difference between a real thaler and an ideal thaler is not merely conceptual, but makes all the difference, as we have already said, between having and not having, to such an extent that, in order to get something real out of the ideal thaler, it made sense to settle for a quarter of the nominal value of the bill of exchange. In his anti-Leibnizian polemic, Kant is clear on the point:[9] it may well seem like a good question to ask whether the actual is narrower than the possible, to which the answer might be affirmative, given that the actual seems, from a logical point of view, like an additional determination, something that further specifies among the possibilities. Yet, Kant continues, the question is senseless from the ontological point of view, given that, at that level, there is only the actual and there is no merely possible, any more than a lottery ticket equals on its own an actual win.

Let us put the point another way. As a matter of logic, adding existence to something does not add anything interesting from the point of view of what can be known. If I order a plate of *real* spaghetti alla carbonara, I have ordered exactly the same thing I would have ordered if I had asked for simply spaghetti alla carbonara.[10] Thus, the difference between logic and ontology is much sharper than it seemed to Leibniz, for whom the fact that a thing does not exist was not an ontological problem;[11] for being actual is just being possible with something added, namely existence. For Kant, on the other hand, only the actual exists, and it is from there that we must begin: the true point of reference is given by experience, which he regarded as essentially what physics describes.

But this conclusion is not so obvious, and it leads to the Transcendental Fallacy. For it is one thing to say that a possible beer quenches no thirst, and quite another to say that only the things to which physics refers exist. For, in this latter case, there would, for instance, be no professors, but only atoms arranged in professorial shapes, and those shapes themselves would be by no means clearly distinguishable from so many others. We come to this shortly.

Synthetic *a priori* judgments

Let us proceed to Kant's last innovation of a realist bent. In the *theory of reasoning*, Kant invented an entirely new logic, the "transcendental logic," as opposed to the "general logic," which, in Kant's terminology, is what guarantees the validity of arguments.[12] The transcendental logic applies to spatio-temporal experience and is employed by the intellect when it is not concerned solely with itself but is cooperating with sensibility to make an experience possible. Before Kant, no one had ever conceived of a logic of this sort.[13] In particular, no one had ever thought through a family of judgments of the sort that follow from it, namely the synthetic a priori judgments. There are three key moves of elimination and introduction.

1. In the first place, all the **analytic a priori judgments** disappear because Kant shows no interest in writing a dictionary or a logic book. In his view, the problem is one of building up a system of the principles of the intellect as they apply to experience insofar as they make that experience itself possible. The Principle of Non-contradiction (which Kant takes to be the prime example of an analytic judgment) does not make experience possible; at best, it allows us to avoid fallacious arguments.[14] On the other hand, the thesis that the "I think" must be capable of accompanying all our representations (Kant's prime example of a synthetic judgment) does render experience possible.[15] Hence, this will be the thesis that founds the new logic, unseating the Principle of Non-contradiction, which had until then dominated, not just as a law of thought but also as a norm for reality.[16]

2. In the second place, there are no **synthetic a posteriori judgments** of the sort that filled the empiricists' treatises of human nature. As the empiricists themselves admitted and

Kant insisted, these judgments are too chancy to find a place in a genuinely certain scientific treatment. As for Descartes,[17] so for Kant, real science is what is indubitable and evident. For Kant, moreover, this means what is mathematizable, and the consequence is that psychology and chemistry are not genuine sciences.[18]

3. Thus we come to the curious family of **synthetic a priori judgments**. Kant's invention of these starts from the consideration that all the judgments of mathematics are of this sort.[19] They form the presuppositions without which we could not have experience, and they do not derive from it. They are not subject to the uncertainties of experience because they are necessary, and they put us in touch with reality, which is the only thing Kant cares about in ontology. Because mathematical judgments are secure but do not constitute knowledge, because they are mere thoughts, Kant's efforts are directed at transforming some of the judgments that the empiricists classified as synthetic a posteriori (the five ontological principles of the "I," of Space, Time, Substance, and Cause) into synthetic a priori, giving them a foundation in the certitudes of physics.

Are synthetic *a priori* judgments possible?

Kant's move is nevertheless high risk and would have seemed reckless had it not been supported by his confidence in physics. Are synthetic a priori judgments possible in metaphysics? Let us follow through the steps.

1. As regards **arithmetic**, Kant holds that the proposition "7 + 5 = 12" is a synthetic judgment because 12 is necessarily thought of neither in the concept of 7 nor in the concept of 5, for we may arrive at it by way of 8 + 4 or 6 + 6; but it is an a priori judgment because we do not arrive at it by way of experience, for instance, by counting objects or using our fingers, because in that case we would not be able to account for additions of larger numbers, it being implausible to suppose that we get to "7,541 + 5,471 = 13,012" by counting on our fingers or by scrutinizing piles of objects.

2. The same holds for **geometry**: geometers do not describe, but construct.

3. Kant uses the models provided by arithmetic and geometry to arrive at his first two metaphysical theses: **space** is considered as a priori and naturally geometrical, and **time** is adopted as a priori and naturally arithmetic, though the connection between time and arithmetic is not as forcefully enunciated as that between space and geometry.

4. As regards **physics,** Kant is utterly convinced that principles such as the permanence of **substance** and as **causation** cannot be derived from experience. Hence, physics and its successes provide the basis on which Kant can found his two theses of substance and cause, which are of the first importance for him in his anti-empiricist polemic.

5. Finally, the naturalization of physics by means of metaphysics is carried through by the introduction of the **I think**, which was obviously no concern of the physicists, who dedicated themselves to an objective description of nature rather than to a justification of knowledge. Kant's underlying idea is that the "I" cannot be a mere support or blank page on which sensations are written, but it must constitute the unity without which experience cannot be had.

As we can see, the possibility of synthetic a priori judgments is the public face of the naturalization of physics at the core of the transcendental philosophy. For Kant, the five ontological theses are not just the hypotheses of a philosopher (or, for space, time, cause, and substance, the hypotheses of a scientist); they are rather the ways in which any being like us is related to the world.[20]

Dogmas of empiricism, dogmas of transcendentalism

Having set out Kant's novelties, I would like now to draw the reader's attention to a slightly subtle point.

After reading the first *Critique* for a while, we can't help raising an obvious question about the difference between "all bodies are extended," which Kant treats as the paradigm of an analytic a priori judgment, and "all bodies have weight," which appears as an example of a synthetic a posteriori judgment. Kant's thought is that being extended is a property implicit in the concept "body," whereas the fact of having weight depends on experience, because we must have encountered a body to be in a position to say that it has weight.

The issue is controversial on at least two grounds. In the first place, in Kant's day there were lots of people who thought that some bodies could be unextended.[21] And, second, in the absence of gravity a body is weightless. *It would thus seem that we need at least experience of a body to know that it is extended, and that experience of a body might not inform us that it has weight.*

On the basis of observations of this sort, the American philosopher Willard van Orman Quine (1908–2000)[22] sought to do away with the analytic–synthetic distinction, claiming that it was a mere dogma. You find analytic judgments in dictionaries and synthetic ones in encyclopedias, yet the lexicographers who write dictionaries are no less empirical scientists than are those who write encyclopedia articles. Which is to say that everything we know, even if it were just that no bachelor is a married man, calls for a cognitive basis that is not to be found in the heaven of reasoning but on the earth of knowledge.

The point of this argument was first put forward by the German philosopher Friedrich Adolf Trendelenburg (1802–1872), who noted that the analytic–synthetic distinction boils down to the difference between what we have long known, and so seems analytic, and what we don't know or have only recently learned, and so seems synthetic.[23] The distinction itself is empirical and in no way transcendental. A slightly inexact example might clarify the point: a proposition like "smoking kills," which we find on every packet of cigarettes, might be happily regarded as analytic, though fifty years ago, or at least until it was added to the packets, it would have rather been counted as synthetic.

Thus both the Leibnizians and the empiricists went wrong in thinking they could separate the necessary a priori propositions of logic from the contingent a posteriori propositions derived from experience. For our purposes, what matters is that Quine's argument against the analytic–synthetic distinction applies equally well to Kant's differentiation of synthetic a priori judgments and synthetic a posteriori ones. After all, the former do not constitute logical primitives, but merely reflect the specific state of science in his day.

How can it be that Kant did not take account of this and did not wonder whether his synthetic a priori of the "I," substance, cause, time, and space might not be just an abstraction of some physical principles?

And the answer must be that he was utterly convinced of the identity between physics and experience, and between physics and logic. And this led him, on the one hand, to describe our experience in the same terms as science, and, on the other, to assume that the principles of physics were not derived a posteriori from the current state of human knowledge, but laid down a priori in our conceptual makeup. It is a historical irony that it is precisely in committing this fallacy that Kant's philosophy has been an unchallenged success.

5

———

The Transcendental Fallacy
(Examination)

A semi-catastrophe

The success of Kant's fallacy gives food for thought, for not one of the platypuses to which he gave birth had an easy life.[1]

The more academically inclined Leibnizians accused Kant of extravagance or, in the alternative, of banality. They held that he had done nothing except make unwieldy and obscure what in Leibniz was a clear as daylight.[2] Reactions such as these gave Kant occasion for replies that were sometimes polemical and sometimes even amusing.[3] Popular and anti-academic philosophers[4] were not far wrong in seeing in Kant the source of the nihilism that would shortly grow up, because, in the long run, transcendentalism ends up doing away with the world of the "I." Scholars of history and of languages, who were given to supposing that they were the curators of the true transcendental, accused Kant of having ignored them and thus set on foot a fine tradition that has lasted two centuries.[5] And Roman Catholic commentators dug up all the contradictions hidden in the search for pure sensible intuitions and in the dependence of thoughts on a transcendental "I think."[6]

Outside the narrowly philosophical realm, the mathematicians declared him incompetent and threw doubt on the idea that mathematical judgments were synthetic.[7] And the physicists, the other great model of the Copernican revolution, would always give him his formal due of praise, but it would be the changes in physics that would put on the defensive an approach that depended essentially on absolute concepts of space and time, which themselves became untenable after the theory of relativity.

Among Kant's own followers, the realists[8] and the physiologists[9] accused him of idealism. The idealists were impatient with the timidity of his reforms and with his not having gone further with the principles

43

that the world is constructed out of the "I,"[10] so much so that Kant had to distance himself from their interpretations of him.[11]

In short, a semi-catastrophe that, to do him justice, never undermined Kant's standing. Nevertheless, as I have hinted, his grossest fallacy long remained unnoticed, just like the purloined letter of Edgar Allan Poe (1809–1849),[12] precisely because it was too obvious.

The purloined letter

Hume had made science depend on experience and concluded that science is only probable. Kant reverses the point of view and bases the certitude and necessity of experience on the fact that it is founded a priori on science.

For all that it is expressed in an exaggerated form, the interesting point here is the underlying continuity between Kant and the dominant tradition in philosophy to regard science and experience as two extremes that are wholly interchangeable: science is experience made that bit more refined and systematic, and experience is science that lets itself go and is available to everyone. This was an assumption that was all the easier to allow given that, in Kant's day, the two spheres were that much closer and no one would have thought to propose a distinction between descriptive and prescriptive metaphysics, between the world as it appears to naive common sense and as it really is when seen, for instance, through an electron microscope.[13]

As we shall see at length in Chapters 9 and 10, the transcendental deduction, according to which the conditions for the possibility of an object are just the same as the conditions for the possibility of its being known, is a systematic employment of the fallacy, which I call such because it sets the scene for the consequences in the way that Kant's inquiry develops and, so, for the shape of subsequent philosophy.

A mind-dependent world

There are four things that follow from this (though they do not really follow logically).

1. The fallacy makes a thing depend on the way that it is known. Here, "knowing" means having an experience that is more or

less science, though it is obviously not so given that we can perfectly well *encounter* a thing without knowing it, that is, without having the slightest idea of its internal properties and without being able to identify it. When the citizens of Metropolis look into the sky and exclaim, "It's a bird! It's a plane! It's Superman!," it is clear that they can see *something* without knowing with any precision *what*.[14] If we set this sort of case aside, we would have to say that we see something only when we know it, which is plainly false, though Kant generally seems to think that this is what happens.

2. The phrase "not how things are in themselves, but how they must be if they are to be known by us" is multiply ambiguous because "know" can mean (a) the operations carried out, unbeknownst to us in the process of knowing the external world, by our senses and our categories; (b) the form taken by our senses and our nervous system as an architecture for knowledge; or (c) what we know as experts.

3. In any case, we end up with a reduction of objects to the subjects that know them. And this reduction can be read in differing ways according to how we conceive the role of subjectivity in it.[15] In the most extreme version, the way is open to transcendental idealism, which need not be in the manner of a Berkeleyan identification of *esse* and *percipi* as much as the apparently more cautious *esse est concipi*, which turns out to be more pervasive and insidious: things exist only insofar as we consciously represent them to ourselves, with a consciousness that likewise constitutes the primary foundation of science.

4. It is primarily in the Aesthetic and the Analytic, where Kant discusses what is accessible to experience, that the fallacy comes into view, but it is nevertheless present also in the Dialectic. For Kant, the physics of his day made it obvious that questions of God, the soul, and the world could not be decided in any conclusive way, so that, for instance, whether the world had a beginning in time or not could not be decided. But in the twentieth century just this sort of question would be the subject of scientific discussion; thus, contrary to what Kant thought, the unknowability in question is not absolute

but subject to history.[16] Of course, this is not to criticize
Kant for not having been a prophet, but merely to stress that,
with the passage of time, what he had naturalized returned
to being historicized.

An avoidable fallacy

Could the fallacy have been avoided? Perhaps in Kant's day it could not
have been, but the twentieth century could have done better. However,
if lies get found out in the long run, the run is no longer for fallacies.

One good way of bringing it out into the open has been proposed
by the American philosopher John Searle (b. 1932).[17] Reality is made
up of a shared Background for our theories, and it is a mistake to blur
the difference between, on the one hand, the variety of our measuring
systems and conceptual schemes and, on the other, what they refer to. It
is a creeping nonsense to suppose that conceptual relativism implies anti-
realism, but it is nonsense on stilts to suppose that Searle cannot weigh
at the same time 160 pounds and 73 kilograms. Searle's strategy, in line
with a deep tradition in modern philosophy,[18] is to stress the difference
between what there is and the ways in which we know what there is.[19]

An alternative approach may nevertheless be preferable for present
purposes, one that does not do without the appeal to reality as Background and to primitive certainties, but that has, in my view, the advantage of bringing to the fore the inadequacies of Kant's formulation of
the scientific theory as a description of experience. Let us agree that
thinking of a thing is one thing and knowing it another. But we also
have to agree that knowing a thing is not the same as encountering it,
for instance, banging into a chair in the dark. And, however our experience might become, we must admit that most of it has this opaque and
incorrigible undertow, where the conceptual schemes that organize our
knowledge count for very little.

In an earlier book, I suggested that the naturalization of physics
calls for the basic level to be counted as ontology and the higher as
epistemology.[20] But I do not mean to repeat that theory here, but to use
it to show Kant's confusion between the two levels by means of a simple
litmus test. The studies that the twentieth century carried out (and the
total absence before should be a cause for reflection) in "naive physics,"[21]
concerning the ways in which an experience is often in conflict with what
we know or believe about things, offer clear, but often unintentional,
evidence against the Kantian equivalence.

The strategy of Chapters 6 through 8, in which I take on Kant's basic claims and seek to show their shortcomings as accounts of experience, and not of science, aims to set out this question and to examine Kant's proposals regarding conceptual schemes, phenomena, space, time, the "I," substance, and cause, with a view to seeing whether they really suffice to explain our experience.

Conceptual Schemes and Phenomena

Over-powerful spectacles

Let us return to the main story. In Chapter 2, I said that the theses of conceptual schemes and of the phenomena were "epistemological" insofar as they concern the most general features of the way in which we know the world through the Copernican revolution. As we saw, Kant's basic view is that without the sort of spectacles that the conceptual schemes constitute, we would not have orderly intuitions, and that intuitions that we receive through the lenses of the concepts are, obviously enough, not things-in-themselves but phenomena, that is, things that *seem* to us in a certain way. And the way in which they seem to us is precisely the outcome of two distinct organizations. On the one hand, there is our sensory makeup: we see ultraviolet rays, but not infrared; our experiences are always spatio-temporal; telepathy does not occur. On the other hand, there is our conceptual apparatus: we divide reality up into objects thanks to Substance; we recognize sequences thanks to Cause; and we refer our experiences to the "I."

In part, Kant's claim is perfectly reasonable. Nevertheless, it is presented in so extreme a form as to make it an easy target for refutation. Which is what we do in this chapter, showing (1) that the thesis of conceptual schemes in the strong form that Kant espouses is unsustainable; and (2) that the thesis of the phenomena is incoherent. Thus we use primarily empirical arguments against the former and logical ones against the latter.

The Thesis of Conceptual Schemes

The extremism of the Thesis of Conceptual Schemes, according to which "intuitions without concepts are blind," follows directly from the transcendental fallacy. To do science no doubt concepts are necessary, but a range of perplexities can be raised about whether they are necessary for experience.

The first perplexity is a question of whether the facts are really so. Are intuitions really blind without concepts? This is not the trivial matter of pointing out that I can run into something I didn't expect, or of which I don't have a concept. Rather, what is at stake is the observation that I can be in pretty complex visual states without being able to recognize what is in front of me. This may happen, for instance, when I see a component from inside a vacuum cleaner without having an idea of what it is. Or, conversely, I can have a concept without my intuitions coming up to scratch. And this happens with the Müller-Lyer illusion reproduced below, in which the lines are of the same length, for all that they continue to look different to me:

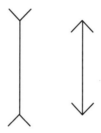

Figure 6. The Müller-Lyer illusion

It would be to argue in a circle to claim that I need the concepts "equal" and "unequal" in order to grasp the apparent inequality. Or, rather, it would be an absurdity that can be made apparent by the analogue claim that, to see a color, I need the concept of "color" or, worse, the concept of the exact color I have before me.

Lurking behind the factual question there is a more serious theoretical and linguistic issue of how, exactly, "concept" and "conceptual scheme" are to be interpreted. Do we have to do with clear and distinct ideas? With a word? With a physiological, perhaps neurological, system? With a conscious schema? In all likelihood, this last is what Kant had in mind, in the light of the Thesis of the "I think," though the others often seem to be in play in various connections. Kant is not to blame for this confusion: he inherits it. When Descartes maintains that unless we have a concept of "wax" we cannot not establish the continuity of the sweet-smelling solid and the odorless liquid, he is following the same line of thought.[1] Likewise Locke, when he responds that the King of Siam could not believe the Dutch ambassador's tale that in winter in his country, water could become solid enough to sustain an elephant.[2] Descartes supposes that identity is furnished by the concept, underestimating the times, including his time of writing, when he sees a candle burn down; on the other hand, to save the power of habit, Locke forgets that we may never have actually seen a puddle freeze over and that experience tells us only that where there was water there is now ice.

This is just the point. It would have been much easier to explain the recognition of identity through transformation by appeal to sameness of spatial place, the sameness that makes us suppose, rightly, that a butterfly can come out of a chrysalis, and, wrongly, that worms are generated by the decay of meat. In other words, Descartes' conceptual criterion of identity is too strong and seems to require knowledge of inner workings of things, but Locke's response seems too weak and would lead us to claim that we would not register transformations if experience had not habituated us to recognize them. In many ways, the idea that intuitions without concepts are blind is still part of this presupposition, which in turn derives from the indeterminacy of the concept of a "concept."

And this is not a mere matter of words. Behind the linguistic problem there lurks the altogether vaster difficulty of the whole claim of Conceptual Schemes.[3] The idea is that we have no access to the external world without appeal to schemes. But this is less than obvious, because, to prove it, we would have to appeal to an impossibility, namely seeing what happens to a subject who is without conceptual schemes.[4] What we can, however, show is that we are very frequently able to explain the way we navigate the world without appealing to schemes and that, as in the case of two Müller-Lyer lines above, what we see is in conflict with what we think. It is thus possible to reply in too many ways to the question of the necessity of the categories of experience, saying that we need 12 or 120 or 1,200 or, indeed, none.

Quite apart from objects' dependence on subjects,[5] the objects are also determined by scientific theories that are not merely explanatory but also constitutive of them. Suppose that a metaphysician who is open to physics establishes that the identity of an object is fixed by the state of the particles that make it up; in that case, a rundown battery is a different object from a charged one. Suppose, on the other hand, that a metaphysician who is open to the neurosciences decides that the world depends essentially on the configuration of our brains; in that case, he should conclude that for a patient presenting with right parietal lesions, half of space really is missing.[6]

Are intuitions without concepts blind?

All the same, it looks as though the claim that intuitions without concepts are blind, which is the argument that sets conceptual schemes at center stage, is not without resources.

The first and most obvious of these concerns cultural constructs. Let us take a piece of writing like the following:

SHADOW

Figure 7. Shadow foreshadowed

It's not hard to suppose that an illiterate (or merely someone who knows no English) would not be able to decipher what is written and, so, would not recognize the shadows.[7] But it is fairly clear that there is something weak about calling on reading as a case in which concepts feed into intuitions. For it is obvious that reading is a conceptual task, one in which seeing has a subordinate role.

Nevertheless, historians of art, such as Gombrich,[8] offer other cases in which we have the reproduction of physical objects, rather than writing about them. A German pen and ink drawing of 1540 shows Castel Sant'Angelo in Rome as having gothic features; Matthäus Merian's seventeenth-century rendering of Notre Dame de Paris makes it out to have baroque elements; Dürer's rhinoceros is a queer beast that has very little to do with the animal we see at the zoo; a cityscape of Naples painted by a Tuscan artist makes the famously white roofs out of red Florentine tiles; in eighteenth-century drawings, North American Indians looks decidedly rococo. For all that such examples might be more impressive, they do not offer definitive proof because they all turn merely on the issue of how habit (and not Kant's a priori schemes) can interfere with perception. Consider trying to reproduce a signature. As anyone who has tried to forge one knows, signatures involve expressive habits that are very hard to suppress or interfere with. Kant's claim, however, is that perception does not take place without conceptual schemes. But, far from being refuted, this is actually confirmed by the art historian's examples: despite the greater or lesser aberrations, what we see is still a rhinoceros, an Indian, the Castel Sant'Angelo, Notre Dame, and Naples.

For their part, psychologists adduce other evidence, which seems to go deeper.[9] Irrespective of cultural background, even very small children tend to project recognition schemes onto things.[10] And it is possible to show that vision is not a passive registering, but an active operation. In one experiment, subjects are asked to draw a certain meaningless shape from memory.[11] Some reproduced—or rather *interpreted*—the shape in question as a pickax, accentuating the point; others took it for an anchor and brought out its characteristic features. Only one subject reproduced it correctly, after having identified it as a Stone Age hatchet. Which might seem to point to the idea that, where we have no preexisting category, there is no way to avoid deformation. But does this really mean that intuitions without concept are blind? Or only that concepts *can intervene* in intuitions?

Clearly, the latter. And this is a perfectly reasonable claim, but not one that Kant would care about because it assigns too modest a role to conceptual schemes. It is entirely plausible to recall that when Marco Polo first saw a rhinoceros, he interpreted it as a unicorn, making the real unknown into a known unreal.[12] There is no problem about all this because the point is deeper seated. For Kant, what is at stake is not whether concepts guide intuitions, especially when we have to do with recognition and reproduction, but the claim that without concepts we are blind, and that the sphere of the visible (and, in general, of the perceptible) is totally determined by the conceptual. Which is plainly not so.

What, for instance, do we see in the description of the Odradek in the story "A Father's Worry" by Franz Kafka (1883–1924)?

> At first, it looks like a flat, star-shaped rocket, and it seems to be covered in wire; these could only be old wires that have been pulled out. But it is not just a rocket; from the center of the star a small stick pokes out sideways, to which is attached a second at right angles. By means of this latter projection and one of the rays of the star, the whole thing can stand up straight as if on two legs. One might be led to think that once the shape had a more rational form, and now it is simply broken. But this seems not to be the case; at least nothing indicates that it is; there are neither joints nor traces

of breakage. On the other hand, it is hard to say more because the Odradek is very mobile, and it is impossible to catch it.[13]

Kafka goes on for many lines describing a thing of which neither he nor we have any concept (or, rather, the slightest idea). Which is the whole point. And the moral is that, at the perceptual level, we don't construct anything whatsoever with our conceptual schemes. For instance, we don't construct the chessmen or the chessboard, but only, what is a whole other kettle of fish, the game of chess. And it is a blessing that this is so; otherwise we would find ourselves in a phantasmagorical world in which, as Nietzsche the extreme Kantian claimed, there are no facts, only interpretations.[14]

Recognizing that there are non-conceptual contents in an intuition is an indispensable step toward giving conceptual schemes their proper role.[15] But Kant's extremism prevents him from doing precisely this. In the face of so lapidary a claim as "intuitions without concepts are blind," there is nothing to be done but reply.

1. **We can see even without concepts**. The spots reproduced below are not easily conceptualizable, and even calling them "spots" isn't yet to have a concept of them. Yet we have no difficulty individuating their positions and interrelations.

Figure 8. Seeable spots

2. **We can have concepts yet not see**. The groups of triangles reproduced below are identical in their shape, direction, and disposition of the elements within each group. Yet we see them as different.

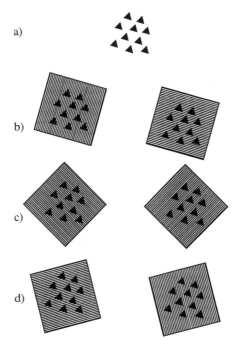

Figure 9. Various triangles

3. **Intuitions without concepts can see perfectly well**. The possibility of having complex visions without understanding the nature of what is being perceived is precisely what happens in people blind from birth who have been operated on as adults at the end of a process of visual rehabilitation. From the point of view of physiology, we can be sure that they distinctly see what they have in front of them, but that they can't understand exactly what they are seeing, as is proved by their need to use the sense of touch.[16]

4. **Seeing a duck-rabbit**. A final point. There is a sense in which the Thesis of Conceptual Schemes can be maintained that is not the obvious and acceptable sense given to it in epistemology. It is just that Kant never thought of it. This regards the language we use to *describe* our experiences, rather than to have them.[17]

Figure 10. Jastrow's duck-rabbit

Although I can know that both are present, it is a fact that I cannot see both the duck and the rabbit at the same time. It might be argued that this depends on what I am like rather than what a duck-rabbit is like. But it primarily has to do with what it is to see. And it is only in this sense, which in turn is not so much connected, as Kant would claim, to the physiology of perception, as it is to the grammar and the semantics of the words and sentences we use,[18] that one might defend the thesis that "intuitions without concepts are blind." If someone were to see both the rabbit and the duck at the same time, then the verb "to see" would take on quite a different meaning from the one we normally give it.

Are concepts without intuitions empty?

We come now to the converse thesis, that concepts without intuitions are empty. In Kant's way of setting things up, this assertion comes out as a triviality that is the direct consequence of the idea that concepts are like spectacles superimposed on experience: if there is nothing to see, you see nothing except the spectacles. But this is not the only way to take the notion of a concept. For it can easily be considered as itself an *object*, albeit an ideal one. In that case, a concept without an intuition can be fully saturated. If the concept of a triangle has a value, it does so because it possesses properties independently of any subject thinking of or knowing it. Otherwise, the discovery of the properties of a triangle would be an exercise in introspective psychology. As a result, it is not true that concepts without intuitions are empty: I can have perfectly formed concepts of things that I shall never encounter in intuition, as a matter of fact (a golden mountain), as a matter of logic (a round square), or, perhaps, both (the highest prime number).[19] The same applies to fictional characters: what color eyes does Lucia Mondella have in Manzoni's *The Betrothed*? Or merely to historical characters: how many readers can think about what Metternich looked like? Or again to distant places: all I know about Auckland is that it is the capital of New Zealand, and no monument, landscape, or restaurant comes to mind. But in these cases, my *cognitio cæca* (blind knowledge) is quite enough, at least for my present purposes.

The Thesis of the Phenomena

Having gone through the conceptual schemes, we come now to the Thesis of the Phenomena, which corresponds to them at the level of sensibility. As a rough guide, it seems acceptable enough, but upon closer scrutiny things change. Whereas in the case of the conceptual schemes, the problems were primarily empirical, here the difficulties are logical. What are we really referring to when we believe that we are referring to a phenomenon and not a thing-in-itself, *once we have asserted that we know only phenomena?*

Here is where the major conceptual difficulty lies. For we must distinguish between (1) asserting that a rainbow is a phenomenon and a chair is a thing, and (2) holding that just as much as the rainbow, so also the chair, and any other thing in space and time or merely in time, like consciousness, is a phenomenon. Where (1) looks like a typical piece of common sense, (2) is a typical move of the Copernican revolution. Now, it doesn't take much thought to see that common sense, which lets us use perceptual verbs like "to see," "to feel," and so on without any hint of skepticism, is much smarter than the Copernican revolution and avoids many useless headaches.

This can be shown easily. At a certain point Kant writes:

> The predicates of the phenomenon can be ascribed to the object itself, in relation to our sense, for instance, the red color or the scent to a rose. But what is illusory can never be ascribed as predicate to an object (for the sufficient reason that we then attribute to the object, taken by itself, what belongs to it only in relation to the sense or in general to the subject), for instance, the two handles that were formerly attributed to Saturn.[20]

Apart from the fact that Saturn really does have rings, this way of putting things raises at least three questions:

1. Why do things have to be different from the way they seem? Experience shows that sometimes they are. But in the great majority of cases, they are not. It is exactly for this reason that the distinction between appearance and reality is a prime piece of our conceptual furniture. And if we conceded everything Kant wants, we would have, in the end, to do away with it.

2. Why distinguish things from their representations? When I see a rose in front of me, I do not think that I have a mere content of consciousness, as I might when I think that I might give it to someone. At the time that I am looking at the rose, my representation also implies that the rose is out there, whether it is being represented or not.

3. And, above all, if the red is not in the rose, where is it? Like the *eidola* or simulacra of the Epicureans, which were images that peel off things and hit our eyes to produce knowledge, Kant's phenomena seem to be suspended literally in midair, being neither in the subject nor in the object. But we have never seen simulacra or phenomena wandering about the streets in midair.

We will hear it objected that there is nothing queer about saying that the red is not (only) in the rose. After all, it turns out to be distributed at least among (a) the physical constitution of the petal; (b) the wavelength of light that the petal reflects; and (c) the observer who registers it and determines the perceptual contents.[21] It is at this point, however, that we no longer understand where the red *is*, spread out a bit in the head, a bit in things and a bit in between, so that saying "this pen is red" comes to seem a misleading way of talking and to demand that we reform our language.[22]

Moreover, elsewhere Kant talks as if red were an objective property of things. For instance,[23] he observes, quite rightly, that if cinnabar were sometimes red and sometimes another color, then our world would be chaotic and disorderly. But how could this be if, in the end, colors are in us? Kant's theory does not allow us to answer, or even to raise, questions like: What difference is there between perceiving and *imagining* perceiving? Between looking at a watch and *thinking about* a watch? This is not a trifling omission, given that it carries with it in the long run the disappearance of the objective world. For the objectivity it leaves is the kind to which someone might appeal, to show the truth of some fact, by buying two copies of the same newspaper that, obviously enough, carry the same news. This works only up to a certain point: try it and see.

Space and Time

What is the Transcendental Aesthetic?

Having considered the epistemological doctrines, we move to examine the theses regarding Space and Time. Kant deals with these in the section called "Transcendental Aesthetic," a title that might sound strange to us, accustomed as we have been over the last two centuries to associate aesthetics with the philosophy of art. As we have seen, Kant takes "aesthetics" in its etymological sense of "sensibility," the realm in which sensations are registered, just as logic is the sphere of the production of thoughts. Now, when I see a rose, I acknowledge it in space and time, and there are no other dimensions. These, then, are the two great axes of the transcendental aesthetic. This much seems fairly intuitive. Indeed, Kant does not regard the isolation of Space and Time as the pure forms of intuition as particularly problematic. So much so that he had formulated the basic claims eleven years before the publication of the *Critique of Pure Reason*.[1] And the theses in question are easy to swallow because they are not much at odds with common sense.

For the austere or minimalist interpretation offered by Strawson,[2] the two theses of the transcendental aesthetic merely assert that any coherent experience must possess some temporal ordering and that many experiences are disposed in spatial order. But Kant himself is not so moderate. As regards both Space and Time, he wants to demonstrate much more, and specifically that:

1. Space and time are a priori, that is, independent of experience;

2. They are *transcendental*, that is, they make experience possible;

3. They are *intuitions* that are singular and immediate rather than universal and mediated concepts.[3]

Space

Let us look first at what Kant has to say about space.

As regards its being a priori, the priority of space relative to objects is defended on the grounds that we can think of space without objects, but we cannot think of objects without space. Clearly, Kant has not raised the question of whether it is possible to think of a space without at least some color; hence, he argues for his claim on the basis of an over-rich notion of an "object."[4] Moreover, Kant's thesis aims to stress the dependence of space on the characteristics of the pure subject. But if it is objected that space possesses at least one color (including, of course, black and white), we notice that this law applies entirely to the object.

Proceeding to the transcendental nature of space, the claim is that pure space should make possible our experience of objects. It is obvious that what is being postulated is a perfect coincidence between geometry, as the guarantee of the certainty of experience, and perception, as the means by which we have experience of the world. But, as in the case of the refutation of the metaphysical thesis, this assumption does not hold. This is the case not for a priori reasons, but as a matter of fact: perceptual space does not coincide with that of Euclidean geometry and, as geometers, we are either under-endowed or over-endowed for Euclidean geometry.

The case of specular opposites makes the point eloquently. And it is all the more interesting for having been discussed several times by Kant himself,[5] without his having drawn the consequences for his own theory. If we really were naturally and exclusively Euclidean geometers, we would not be able to recognize the identity of shapes that cannot be superimposed, such as the right hand and the left hand, or two triangles inscribed on two hemispheres. In such cases, we cannot appeal to the simple proof of the identity of the two shapes by superimposing one on the other: remember that two hands clasped are not superimposed; whether by hook or by crook, you will find that they cannot be really made to superimpose.

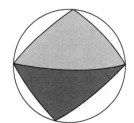

Figure 11. Specular triangles

In point of fact, we grasp the sameness of shape without overlaying one on the other; in this sense, we are over-endowed as Euclideans. In other cases, we regard as plausible solids shapes that in fact are not so. The picture below does not depict a possible object with only one face hidden, though generally we recognize this only once we have been told; in this sense we are under-endowed geometers.

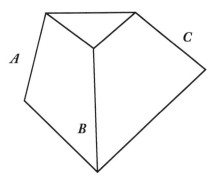

Figure 12. Vertex

To get clear about the claim that Space is an intuition and not a concept, we must make a distinction. *Geometrically*, space is indeed an intuition, or may be regarded as such. But *ecologically*, that is, in terms of how we deal with experience, we have to do with various different spaces: open or closed, bird's eye or worm's eye, mental or real. These are then gathered, as empirical cases, under the general concept of "space."[6] And this goes in spades as a matter of *physiology*: someone who has suffered a right parietal lesion is literally lacking one-half of his perceptual experience, half of the space, so that he or she will eat only one-half of a dish and will put on only half a coat.[7] At this level, the construction of space is paradoxically much more similar to the claim made about the constitutive role of concepts in experience than it is to the theses of the transcendental logic.

Time

We come now to Kant's claim that time is a priori, that is, that the pure form of time precedes and includes any temporal experience. Is this really so? Would we perceive time in the absence of movement and change?

After all, the claim that if we didn't have a sense of time, we wouldn't perceive movement does not seem any stronger than the converse claim that without movement, we wouldn't experience time. The position seems to be similar to that of the supposed priority of space relative to objects, and Kant's thesis is improperly supported as much by the alleged impossibility of a world without time as it is by the variety of ways in which the word "time" is deployed.

As regards the impossible experiment, we can also in this case attribute to the objects the a priori feature that Kant attributes to time as the form of the inner sense. For instance, we might appeal to the fact, already noticed by Aristotle,[8] that time appears phenomenologically to depend on the movements of objects in the external world. Trivially, in sensory deprivation or merely by staying still in a dark room for a period, one loses the sense of time. But Kant requires it to be always as active as the "I think" with which one identifies oneself.

As to the second point, it is not hard to bring out the ambiguities and multiplicity of meanings that Kant attaches to the word "time." In some places, it is the sense of what is outside us. In others, it is the inner flux of our consciousness. And in still others, it is nothing but that consciousness itself. But this is a further hidden confusion that can be laid bare by citing an analogy. If we were to use the word "pizza" to apply also to borscht, we would have no difficulty in saying that pizza is a traditional Russian dish. Just so, if we were to use "time" to refer to both dawn and dusk, to the fact of being bored or anxious, to mental contents, including spatial representations, then we could happily say that time is everywhere. On this account, time is in the subject, but just because it is made to coincide with it.

We thus come to the claim that time is transcendental, that it is not derived from experiences but rather makes them possible. In fact, time does not seem to be transcendental relative to objects, but only to events. If I say that a table is present, I am asserting its spatial presence; its temporal presence adds nothing. One the other hand, the fall of a leaf necessarily requires time in order to be a fall. Why did Kant not take account of so obvious a point? If we follow through his reasoning, we see that time is much more immediate for us than space is; he does not seem to notice that, in normal conditions, a watch is used much more than a ruler is, which is a hint at the fact that our temporal intuitions are much less well defined than our spatial reckonings. There is, ultimately, a circularity in the reasoning for the claim that time precedes and includes space and intervenes at every point: in order to be known, everything has to be subject to the synthetic unity of apperception, which is the "I" and which is made of time; hence, time has to precede everything else. If, instead of having knowing as our primary objective, we set ourselves to giving ourselves instant pain in the left big toe by stubbing it against a stool, we can be sure that the priority would be handed to space.

From this we can see that Kant handles time both as an intuition (the inner sense) and as a concept (the "I" as consciousness). Hence, the claim that time is an intuition is, once more, supported only by the ambiguous use of the word "time." In any case, the inclusion of space within time is in conflict with Kant's argument against idealism, according to which the perception of a temporal flux in consciousness proves that there is something unchanging outside the "I," namely an external and independent world.[9] Yet again, we find the extreme instability of a concept like "time" (external physical time, the inner sense, the matter of the "I"), and this is why, apparently without having noticed, Kant holds both that the world is inside the "I" and that the "I" is inside the world.

The meaning of mathematization

What is nevertheless of greatest interest for our purposes is Kant's move in transcribing Space as geometry and Time as arithmetic. This is how he prepares to render experience homogeneous and to stamp on it a necessity that will make it safe from the empiricist critique. So far we have a sensible world that has been mathematized and made stable instead of being brute and random. What we still have to understand is whether the intellect really has the a priori principles that are not merely analytic but ampliative. Here, too, mathematics will have the lion's share. But what has to be shown is that there are *judgments* that are at once synthetic and a priori yet are not merely mathematical. These are the judgments of Substance and Cause, which, as such, are not in things, but in the "I" that knows them. These are the three remaining ontological claims that are made in the Analytic, which we now proceed to examine.

Self, Substance, and Cause

Self: The world as representations

With his theory of the subject, Kant stands halfway between Descartes and Edmund Husserl (1859–1938). The "I think" is neither a bare point denuded of positive truth-bearing contents like the Cartesian *cogito*, nor a sphere full of necessary representations—the whole world of phenomena and their laws—like Husserl's Ego. It does not contain very much, but it does contain something, namely the two pure forms of intuition and the twelve categories.

In this way, the "I think" is the mother of all principles, the supreme principle of all synthetic judgments: an experience counts as such by being referred to the "I." We have seen that this assumption underlies the Copernican revolution, and that its omnipresence is in good measure attributable to Kant's systematic confusion of the "I" and time, which reprises the view of St. Augustine of Hippo (354–430), according to which time is not the upshot of the movement of objects in space, but rather of the unfurling ("distension," as Augustine puts it) of the soul.

Kant's claim is, as we have seen, that the whole of space is contained within time, which is in turn the stuff of which the "I" is made.[1] This identification is all the easier for Kant because he doesn't distinguish sharply enough between the "I" and its contents. For him, the following propositions turn out to be of much the same kind:

(1) "I think that 2 + 2 = 4";

(2) "I taste that the coffee is sweet"; and

(3) "I am sad."

But it is fairly clear that (3) is very different from (1) and (2), inasmuch as it is the only expression that, logically, depends on the "I," given that 2 + 2 = 4 and that the coffee is sweet (if it is so) whether or not I think or taste it.

On this basis, we may concentrate on a point we have not yet broached. The thesis that the "I think" constitutes the synthetic unity of representations (Kant says "apperception," meaning conscious perception) implies that everything, from thoughts to memories, from perceptions to hallucinations from what we have in us to what is outside, is a "representation." At a certain point, despite his laudable intent to discriminate the various types of representation, Kant makes this plain:[2]

> The genus is *representation* in general (*repræsentatio*). Subordinate to it stands representation with consciousness (*perceptio*). A *perception* that relates solely to the subject as the modification of its state is a sensation (*sensatio*), an objective perception is *knowledge* (*cognitio*). This is either *intuition* or *concept* (*intuitus vel conceptus*). The former relates immediately to the object and is single, the latter refers to it mediately by means of a feature which several things have in common. The concept is either an *empirical* or a *pure concept*. The pure concept, in so far as it has its origin in the understanding alone (not in the pure image of sensibility), is called a *notion*.

From which we can infer the following classification:

Representations			
Conscious: perception			There are no unconscious representations
Subjective: sensation	Objective: knowledge		
	Intuition (immediate and singular)	Concept (mediated and universal)	
		Empirical	Pure (purely intellectual notions and ideas)

Figure 13. Representations

In line with the thesis of the Phenomena, everything is representation. And, in line with the thesis of the "I think," there is no representation that is not conscious. These are not minor claims: the world is systematically projected onto the screen of the waking mind. Let us now compare Kant's taxonomy with Leibniz's:[3]

Ideas			
Obscure	Clear		
	Confused	Distinct	
		Adequate	Inadequate

Figure 14. Ideas

In Leibniz, obscure knowledge is what we have of something that is perceived but not apperceived; that is, it is not the object of conscious awareness, as might happen when we feel ill at ease with certain persons or situations without being able to account for it (the account might come afterward when we reflect, which shows that those perceptions were present even if not as objects of awareness). This obscure knowledge can become clear when it passes into apperception. In another of Leibniz's examples, a boar has certainly registered the presence of a figure (say, a man) at the end of the field, but it is only when the figure makes a noise that what was latent becomes an apperception and the boar charges in the direction of the stimulus. The boar's clear knowledge may nevertheless be confused: Can it really know that it is attacking a man? This is to be distinguished from distinct knowledge, in which perception is accompanied by a concept, which allows an analysis of the features that form the perception.

  With the due differences, both Kant and Leibniz adopt the same way of classifying what are too generically called "representations." As we can see, Leibniz leaves plenty of room for obscure representations, which are not, properly speaking, perceived—like a toothache that is merely a confused irritation or the single drops of a waterfall. But the Kantian claim that the "I think" must always be able to accompany representations excludes the hypothesis of unconscious representations. Two shortcomings follow from this, one of which is peculiar to Kant, and the other of which is typical of seventeenth- and eighteenth-century philosophy but particularly crippling for a theory of knowledge that gives the leading role to the "I think."

We forget the half of the world that is not representation. Kant is absolutely explicit about this when he sets out the thesis that we know phenomena and never things in themselves. This is all the more problematic when it is applied not to things outside space and time, but precisely to spatio-temporal objects, like a toothache, which present themselves only in fully conscious form and without any phase of latency.

We forget that the world is not a representation. As noted above, Kant's "representation" (like Leibniz's "idea") refers to memories and perceptions, concepts and ideas. And this ends up flattening the distinction between inner and outer, just as the phenomenological features of the world implies—lest we forget—that some things are phenomena and others are not.

Many problems, common, as I have said, to philosophy from Descartes to Kant, follow from the second point, namely the equivalence between the world and its representation. Let us list some of them.

We risk not taking account of the fact that some representations are only in us, whereas others have the feature of being intentionally directed to things outside of us.[4]

We risk ignoring the difference between a perception and a memory, between the sun seen at midday and the sun recalled at midnight, which is such as to make the use of the term "representation" for both improper.[5]

We risk forgetting that an image is static and offers a single point of view, while things can be seen from many vantage points.[6]

A *mental* image exists in the mind and can be modified within certain limits; an *external* image is not an image but a thing that is at a certain distance from the eye. It is not subject to my control and does not depend on me.[7]

Mental images can be either big or small, or neither big nor small.[8]

Mental images have neither smell nor taste.[9]

The image of a needle does not prick and you can't make a call with the image of a telephone.[10]

For sure, we can set all this aside and conclude, as did the consistent Kantian Schopenhauer, that the world is my representation: the world is in my head, and being awake and dreaming are just pages of a single book.[11] But if we take this line, we do not take account of the fact that the world, or, rather, bigger or smaller portions of it, is *represented* in our heads. And the whole of our heads are really in the world.

To show once and for all how little truth there is in the claim of the omnipresence of "representations," I propose a simple experiment for the reader to try, if he or she is wearing glasses. Take them off and move them forward slowly. Up to a certain point (about six inches), you will see two things: an image of the world, our representation of it, and, somewhat fuzzier, the world. This works even without glasses. If you press on your eye with your finger so as to produce a double image, you will not suppose that you have created two objects, but only one object and one ghost image.[12] This is what we risk forgetting with the claim about the "I think." And it is not a minor point, given that, as we shall see in considering the Schematism in Chapter 9, Kant's philosophy finds its most characteristic expression in confusions of this sort. For the time being, we may remark that the two principles that we now consider, of substance and cause, turn out to loom larger as mental contents than Kant would have wanted.

Substance

On an austere account of Kant's doctrine of substance, it would amount to no more than the epistemological principle that objective experience requires that objective temporal relations be set up.[13] But if we look more closely at the thesis that substance involves something's being permanent through time, at least three kinds of problems arise.

Substance is underdetermined in a number of ways. (1) Given that they endure through time, for Kant, holes, shadows, reflections, will-o'-the-wisps, and choruses would all be substances. Both holes and shadows can without a doubt be regarded as metaphysically respectable entities, given that they have identity conditions ("look at that hole on the left," "put yourself in the shadow"),[14] and, given that they are covered by copyright, choruses and symphonies have irrefutable ontological standing. But it is likely that Kant would not agree, given that he held substance to be what were later to be classified as the elements of the periodic table. Moreover, (2) because they both undoubtedly endure in time, both space and time, along with light and many other things, including elevator Muzak, would have to count as substances. Likewise (3) toothaches, obsessions, involuntary memories, names, theorems, and all ideal objects, which would suit many philosophers, but not Kant. In conclusion, (4) Homer's fame, the Roman Empire, and Iago's malice would happily join the substance club. Despite his realistic intentions, the notion of substance that Kant offers gives no criterion for distinguishing one ideal object from another, or a hallucination from a phenomenon.

No precise account is given of what it means to "endure through time" (often enough it seems to amount to "being situated in space"), or how long a thing must endure to count as a substance. And this collapses the distinction between substance and accident: How long does a thing have to last to be a substance rather than an accident?[15]

"Substance" is a chemical or physical definition, and neither an ecological nor an ontological one. Indeed, we never encounter pure substances in experience;[16] moreover, someone who knows nothing about substance can easily witness transformations without supposing there is anything that persists through the change. In other words, if, contrary to Descartes' claim, I can recognize the sameness of wax in its various states without calling in aid the idea of "substance, it is also true that if I witness the passage from liquid to gas in, say, a saucepan left on the fire, it is no consolation that the substance has relocated to mist up the kitchen windows.[17]

The moral is that "substance" does not help me find the soap on the rim of the bath, or to understand that it is soap running down the plughole. For Kant's purposes, the notion is too poor and too rich. Particularly confused and confusing are the ways he identifies substances both with *individuals* and with *objects*. As to the former point, a man, a paper knife, and a Post-it are individuals made up of various substances, which as such are physical or chemical rather than phenomenal, but in that case what use is the schema of substance to recognize a man? As to the latter, we rarely encounter substances in experience, but rather objects that can be long or short, dense or thin, smooth or rough, transparent or opaque. These ontologically salient features are systematically underplayed precisely by Kant's appeal to substance as a physico-chemical characteristic.

Cause

Strawson raises a powerful objection to Kant's thesis about causes,[18] according to which he commits a confusion between a material necessity—which is that there are causes in the world—and an intellectual necessity—which is that we are able to recognize and explain such causes. It remains the case that Kant is better supplied when it comes to the doctrine of causation than with substance. And his argument is that if I shove a piece of chalk with a pencil, the chalk moves. If I didn't have an a priori concept of cause, it is unlikely that I would acquire it from habit, given that what I see is a pencil and a piece of chalk and not a cause.

In the case in hand, then, some science is presupposed of necessity by experience, and this, because a priori, will be a certain cognition. But it is precisely at this point that Kant takes advantage of the many senses of the word "cause." For the pencil causes the movement of the chalk in a very different way from that in which smoking kills or ignorance leads to injustice. In the first case, we have physical contact; in the second, a complex biochemical process; and in the third, a purely intellectual connection. And it is paradoxical that it is the first sort that Kant treats as paradigmatic of the intellect's action on sensibility. It seems to him that it is *visible*, or sensible. This can be illustrated with an anecdote.

In 1943–1944, the psychologist Wolfgang Metzger (1899–1979) was serving as a soldier at Monte Cassino. One day he went to the lavatory in his barracks and, when he was done, pulled the chain. At that exact moment, a grenade hit the barracks, so it seemed to Metzger that his pulling the chain had caused the disaster. If we stick to the level of subjective description, we might say that Metzger *saw* causality, or, to be more neutral, we might say he *perceived* it.

We should not underestimate this anecdote. It is, after all, common enough in experience, not only of Metzger,[19] but also of others.[20] That it was a matter of seeing rather than of thinking can be confirmed by the following consideration. A moment's reflection will show that it is at least odd to suppose that pulling the chain of a cistern will cause an explosion; nevertheless, the impression was immediate, lively, and beyond doubt: that is to say, it carried on its face the evidence normally found in sensible perception. In this sense, Metzger *saw* a cause, even if a split second later he *thought* that it was implausible. It is, therefore, hard to suppose with Kant that causality is a pure principle of the intellect: perceived causality is one thing and it is sensible; thought causality is quite another. The latter is not a principle with which the intellect constitutes experience; at most it explains it sooner or later or perhaps never (was the hole in my jacket caused by a smoking butt or by moths?). But if it *explains* and does not *constitute*, Hume might have been right, and the idea of a cause might be supplied by experience. In fact, not even this can be right. Metzger's experience was of an implausible causality; that is, it was in conflict with everything that experience itself had taught him until then.

Here we have a fine case in which two great philosophers have both got it wrong. Causality is indeed a priori and does not depend on habit. But, at the same time, it amounts to a perceptual capacity,[193] rather than a principle of the pure intellect, in much the same way that our tendency to divide up reality into objects is not, as we have seen, dependent on the intellectual category of "substance."

Now that we have come to the end of Kant's fundamental claims, let us look at the machinery that makes them hum. I beg the reader's patience in the next chapter, but I hope that it will not be a waste of time.

Logical apparatus (Examination)

A complicated contrivance

One classic way of explaining vision is by analogy with the camera obscura. But in the case at hand, it is more helpful to think of a photographic camera. Empiricist theories of experience are rather like fixed-focus cameras, and the transcendental logic seems like an amazingly sophisticated device with loads of commands and complex functions, which is very (indeed, too) hard to use. But our actual experience, being quick and secure and not involving conscious calculations, resembles the most recent foolproof electronic cameras.

Kant's camera, which is a sort of prewar Leica, functions as follows. At the beginning of the cycle, there is the "I," and, at the end, we find Substance and Cause; in the middle, there is a stack of logical and psychological instruments. Judgments, which are the forms of thought posited within the "I," are divided into four families: of quantity (universal, particular, and singular); of quality (affirmative, negative, and infinite) or relation (categorical, hypothetical, and disjunctive); and of modality (problematic, assertoric, and apodeictic). The categories that correspond to them and that are derived by what Kant calls the "metaphysical deduction" are thus also twelve in total, divided into four groups: quantity (unity, plurality, and totality); quality (reality, negation, and limitation), relation (inherence and subsistence, cause and dependence, and community [reciprocity]); and modality (possibility–impossibility, existence–nonexistence, and necessity–contingency). By means of the Transcendental Deduction and the Schematism, the categories are transformed into the principles that regulate experience. In turn, the system of the principles converges on two that are truly basic: Substance and Cause. Here ends the cycle, which, as we shall see, becomes gradually less arcane as we move from judgments to categories and from categories to principles. These last are utterly clear, especially Substance and Cause, which are the only two that Kant really cares about. Here, then, is the scheme:

Judgments	Categories	Deduction	Schematism	Principles	
Quantity Universal Particular Singular	*Quantity* Unity Plurality Totality	Theoretical justification of the application	Physico- physiological justification	*Quantity* Axioms of intuition	
Quality Affirmative Negative Infinite	*Quality* Reality Negation Limitation	of the categories to experience		*Quality* Anticipations of perception	
Relation Categorical Hypothetical Disjunctive	*Relation* Inherence– subsistence, Cause– dependence, Community [reciprocity]			*Relation* Analogies of experience	Substance Cause Reciprocal action
Modality Problematic Assertoric Apodeictic	*Modality* Possibility- impossibility, Existence- nonexistence, Necessity– contingency			*Modality* Postulates of empirical thought in general	

Figure 15. Judgments and principles

It is fairly natural to ask why Kant invested all this time and ingenuity if all he was aiming at was the theses of Substance and Cause. After all, they are just two of the three members of just one family of Principles, those of the Analogy of experience, which in turn corresponds to the categories of Relation.

The explanation seems in the end fairly straightforward. Given the dialectical freight that the theses of Substance and Cause are carrying, because they are independent of experience and make it possible, Kant could not simply appeal to a matter of fact, namely the use that physics suggests we make of them. Rather, in the terms of his naturalization, which is at the heart of the deduction, he had to demonstrate that, for the "I" to have certain experiences, the categories have to be derived from thought, that is, from judgments that are applied by means of the principles. And to do this, he had to, first, take on board what the logicians of his day regarded as the general forms of judgments. And he arrived at twelve of these. Second, he had to derive from them the same number of categories, lest he be accused of picking them up from experience. And, third, he had to manufacture twelve principles from their application that would hold for both science and experience.

As specifically regards the Principles, they are directly influenced by the physics of the Analogies of experience, which themselves reflect the basic positions of Newtonian science. The Principles combine both mathematics and physics not only in the Axioms of intuition, according to which every experience has a number, which is its extension, but also in the Anticipations of perception, according to which every experience has a magnitude, which is its intension. By Kant's explicit admission, the Principles are not concerned with experience, but rather with the relation between the subject and what it knows in the Postulates of empirical knowledge in general; these Postulates correspond to the modal categories of the possible, the necessary, and the actual.

What is really striking in all this is the disproportion between the mass of argumentation and its conclusion. Setting aside that uneconomical use of the means, the real problem is to see whether Kant really reaches his end, namely to demonstrate that his substantive theses really do guarantee the minimum requirements for any experience whatsoever,[1] and not that they merely make up the ingredients of a scientific approach to nature.[2]

Following the analogy with the Leica, it seems the latter. Kant takes himself to be describing an eye, but what he is really setting out are the workings of a camera with a variety of built-in focus meters, light meters, and exposure meters plus a couple of add-on features that don't really do anything. Let us see how this is so.

First Gadget. Judgments and Categories
(Metaphysical deduction)

Kant's first task is to find within the pure "I" the basic forms of judgment, which are independent of and prior to experience, so as then to move to the categories in a movement that, as hinted, Kant calls a "metaphysical deduction,"³ as opposed to a transcendental deduction, which, for simplicity's sake, I have been calling "deduction" tout court. With the categories in place, the judgments can be applied to the concrete organization of spatio-temporal experience, in line with the notion of a "transcendental logic." As against the rationalists, Kant has grasped that concepts are not the minimum unit of meaning, which arises only when a judgment is formulated, that is to say, when a subject is connected with a predicate. "Dog," "runs," and "black" mean nothing; meaning begins when we say "the dog runs" or "the dog is black." Judgment takes place in the "I" and is the result of a category, which organizes the spatio-temporal experience furnished by the transcendental aesthetic.

Kant's underlying assumption is that the unification of experience is effected by the activity of the "I," which, as we saw in the last chapter, is a collector of all representations, or, in other words, is like the film that is exposed. But, contrary to empiricist thought, the process is not passive, insofar as the "I" is given a much stronger unifying role than the blank page or the empty cabinet with which Locke illustrated the nature of experience. The "I" does not merely allow itself to be filled with contents, but it arranges them through the judgments. On Kant's hypothesis, the activity of judging immediately carries with it a categorization, that is, a rational ordering of experience. And this, unlike the story told by Aristotle and traditional metaphysics, does not derive from the characteristics of the objects experienced, but from the rational powers of subjects, that is, the judging activity of the "I."

The first thing that comes to mind in this connection, at least in the light of what we have said about the program of naturalization, is that the Categories do not "follow" from the Judgments as naturally as Kant supposes. Indeed, the whole business seems clumsy and tedious. And it is reasonable to ask why he supposed that the derivation seemed so simple.

The point is that we can allow that judgments determine some categories. But it remains to be seen why they should be those categories rather than others. Given the extreme generality of the judgments, we could instead end up with a table of categories like that imagined by Borges, referring to a supposed Chinese encyclopedia:

> In its remote pages, animals are divided into: (a) belonging to the emperor; (b) embalmed; (c) tame; (d) sucking pigs; (e) sirens; (f) fabulous; (g) stray dogs; (h) included in the present classification; (i) frenzied; (j) innumerable; (k) drawn with a very fine camelhair brush; (l) *et cetera*; (m) having just broken the water pitcher; (n) from a long way off that look like flies.⁴

Thus the question is: How do we get from judgments to Kant's categories and not to Borges's? Kant explains this away by appealing to the fact that judgments are limited and circumscribed by reference to experience. And this is a persuasive move. But Kant does not arrive at it spontaneously, and there are at least two respects in which the process is unwieldy.

When all is said and done, the categories are not derived from judgments the way that Kant claims, but the table is presented as a *rationalization* of the categories already present in the Scholastic tradition. Relative to this, Kant makes two basic changes. On the one hand, he reorganizes the Aristotelian categories, which took no account of the differences between aesthetic and logic and between empirical and transcendental; hence they did not offer pure logical forms.[5] On the other, he fixes twelve as their number with a procedure that, with a fair bout of narcissism, Hegel would praise to the skies as a premonition of the dialectical method of Thesis, Antithesis, and Synthesis. Indeed, each family is made up of three categories, and Kant maintains that the third is the result of combining the first two. Thus, we arrive at an affirmation, a negation, and an intermediate relation. For instance, the judgments of Quality are divided into Affirmative ("the soul is mortal"), Negative ("the soul is not mortal"), and Infinite ("the soul is non-mortal," which Kant counts as different from the preceding because the soul "is located in the sphere of non-mortal beings"[6]). Which amounts to saying, what is not at all obvious, that logic is made both relevant and effective by experience, *though it is independent of it.*

Kant gets out of this difficulty with a second move. It is not experience, but rather science, that leads the dance. The rationalization of the categories goes hand in hand with their *naturalization,* which in turn derives from the Transcendental Fallacy and which again Hegel would summarize in the formula "the Rational is the Real." This whole rigmarole aims at getting to the Principles, which turn out to be those of (Newtonian) physics. And the Principles are then given the job of determining retrospectively the passage from the Judgments to the Categories. For all that it seems that we are moving logically from the Judgments to the Categories and, hence, to the Schemata and the Principles, the real point of departure is with the Principles, from which we arrive at the Schemata, and from there we move backward to the Categories and the Judgments. And we might say that, if we lacked Principles (in accord with physics), then we should be hard put to fix the Judgments and the passage from them to the Categories. After all, it seems no less arbitrary to rise from a Principle like that of Substance to a categorical judgment than it does to descend from a categorical judgment to the "animals belonging to the Emperor."

Second Gadget. Transcendental Deduction

The transcendental deduction has a narrowly theoretically role to play in justifying the application of the categories to experience. That is to say, it is called on to prove not merely that the categories are independent of experience, but that they are an indispensable ingredient of it. To do this, Kant systematically exploits the Transcendental Fallacy.

Strawson rightly observes that the deduction is not just an argument, but also "an explanation, a description, a history."[7] In this way, he emphasizes the strangeness of this part of the *Critique*, which, despite its avowed theoretical intent, mixes together logic, psychology, and epistemology. Kant's declared assumption is that the conditions of possible *knowledge* of the objects of experience are the same as the conditions of possible *experience* of them. With this, Kant commits himself to a thesis that holds good only for a theory of science and not for a theory of experience, and this can be seen in a simple case. For instance, it would be wild to say that a shooting pain in the left arm amounts to even the slightest sort of knowledge, but knowledge might begin with a diagnosis of a heart attack.

Kant's commitment to this confusion comes out most strongly in the first edition of the *Critique*, that of 1781. In the edition of 1787, what we find is a patch of transcendental psychology, a psychology that is stripped of flesh and blood and that is reduced to the individuation of some cognitive functions at a very (or, rather, too) high level. The tensions that lie at the heart of the transcendental logic are concentrated in these pained and painful pages, which cost Kant years of work during the first gestation of the work and then again in the complete rewriting of the passage in the second edition. Let us examine what went on.

Deduction A: Theory of knowledge

In this version, Kant argues that for an object to come to be known, it must first be perceived ("synthesis of perception"), then held in memory or what Kant calls the imagination ("synthesis of reproduction"), and lastly conceptualized ("synthesis of recognition"). In his presentation of it, we have an epistemological argument that isolated the minimal criteria for something's being an experience.[8] Nevertheless, as a description of what happens, the deduction is not entirely convincing. Not only does its emphasis on the role of the "I" in the constitution of reality encourage a Berkeleyan transcendental idealism according to which *esse est percipi*, but it gives rise to a conflict between transcendental idealism and empirical realism. As a transcendental idealist, Kant claims that were it not for the categories, the world would present itself to us as a chaos; but as an empirical realist, he has to say that if the world did not appear stable and orderly, then we would not be able to know it.[9] In this context, Kant speaks of the "synopsis of sense,"[10] which is an otherwise undefined function prior to the three syntheses and which is meant to give a kind of overall picture of the world before the categories come into play.[11] It is therefore hard not to feel the conflict between the constitutive role that is attributed to the categories and one that is merely reconstructive and taxonomical. Kant thus manages to show that knowledge requires categories, which no one would deny, but fails in his more ambitious aim.

Deduction B: Transcendental psychology

In the B edition of 1787, Kant builds on the references to the imagination already present in A as the mediator between perception and intellect. In this way, he puts his argument on a firmer psychological footing and better integrates it with the chapter on the schematism that immediately follows.

The central point of the B version of the deduction is in §24, where Kant sets out his psychological argument virtually appealing to physiological considerations. The idea is that if the unity of an object constitutes also the unity of consciousness in the knowledge of that object, then we should suppose that there is a faculty, the imagination, that mediates between subject and object, unifying the concepts that are in the subject with the sensations that show the presence of the object. Kant insists that this faculty is not merely an empirical and reproductive resource; rather, it is productive inasmuch as it appears to determine the objects by superimposing on them the unification that arises from the intellect. Yet Kant keeps his trump card well up his sleeve[12] in the same way he handles the schematism, as we shall see shortly. The imagination is invoked to give shape to concepts, that is, to produce a figured (*figürlich*) synthesis that colors—we put it this way because in the end it seems to be what Kant has in mind—the intellectual synthesis. The imagination thus colors in the conceptual unification of experience that is guaranteed by the categories.

But there are too many open questions. What is this productive imagination? Who supplies the individual shape (Kant uses the Latin tag *synthesis speciosa*)? Who colors in the shapes? If, on the one hand, colors and shapes come from the intellect, don't we have here something like geometrical construction? If, on the other hand, they come from objects, how can we talk about the imagination's productiveness or about the determining role of concepts? The overall impression is that, even in this version, the deduction plays fast and loose with Kant's threefold understanding of the "I" as time, as the form of the inner sense, and as *cogito*, and that the explanation is merely put off to the schematism.

Third Gadget: The Schematism

Especially in the version of 1781, the deduction answers a question of law: Is it permissible to use logic to determine experience? If so, the Schematism picks up a question of fact: What resources do our minds have that allow them to refer a concept to a percept? And the answer to this is: the schemata. Kant defends three basic theses about these means by which objects are determined by concepts: (1) The schemata are distinct from images; (2) they are methods of construction; and (3) they are forms of time.

With the first of these, Kant resolves one of the besetting problems of empiricism: that of General Idea. As Berkeley had objected to Locke,[13] it is hard to see what the general image of a dog could be. At best, it could be a "diagram," a particular image treated as if it were an instance in the place of other cases. Kant takes up this point and talks of the scheme as a "monogram," an abstract profile.

The second thesis refers to the question of mathematical construction. We begin with concepts and construct them in the imagination as geometers construct shapes. The difference is that where geometers use pure intuition, these constructions must be referred to a percept. There are two sides to this problem. On the one hand, there is the question of *subsumption*, namely the passage from a table to Substance. And on the other, that of *construction*, namely the passage from Substance to a table.

In this way, we arrive at the idea that the schemata are forms of time, that queer thing that is partly in the "I" and partly in the world. Which is generally understood in terms of two fundamental Kantian claims: Substance as permanence, and Cause as succession. The thesis becomes more obscure when we try to apply it, and the obscurities spread backward to the preceding points. To see why, I propose four moves: (1) We ask how the schema works following Kant's indications; (2) we try to integrate those indications with a supplementary hypothesis; (3) we see whether it works; and (4) we show that it cannot work in any case.

How a schema works: Kant's hints

In the austere version, limited to Substance and Cause,[14] the schematism justifies the claim that, contrary to Hume, if we did not have these temporal schemata, our experience would not be possible. Nevertheless, in the chapter given over specifically to the schematism,[15] and in considerations that crop up in the transcendental doctrine of method,[16] Kant makes many claims that do not fit with the austere interpretation. Indeed, they betray an enthusiasm for speculation that anticipates the Idealism of the early nineteenth century. Specifically, there are three troubling features that all derive from the description of the schemata we have just given. These are (1) the reference to the schema as a "monogram," (2) the relation between concept and image, and (3) that between image and empirical instance. These points have in common the fact that they all respond to a much less formal need than that announced by the austere interpretation. Rather, they respond to the need, which is as central for Kant as it is for any theory that aims to explain how concepts refer to objects, to move from the universal to the particular.

Let us look more closely. As we have seen, the schema is a "monogram," that is, Kant explains, it is one of the silhouettes physiognomists used, some black card cut to show a profile, like Puttrich's 1798 drawing of Kant walking. Kant could have referred to shadow puppets or the images projected on the wall of Plato's cave in his effort to make the schema less vague; nevertheless, what we have is a general idea in superficial disguise. From a shadow, we can ascend to a tall man or a short one, to a white man or a black one. But we should note that in the image of the universal as higher and the particular as lower, we are ascending or subsuming and not descending or constructing.

We get the same impression as regards the relation between a concept and an empirical instance. Kant offers the example of the circle and the plate at the beginning of the chapter on the schematism, and he claims that the roundness of the plate makes it homogeneous with the pure geometrical concept of a circle. Yet roundness also applies to many other things, from a wheel to the form of a Parmesan cheese, and the reference to a circle doesn't help much, because it amounts to a rule like "faced with a plate, think of a circle and you'll be OK."

Moving to the question of the relation between image and instance, this feeling gets stronger still when Kant appeals to the schema of a dog, which is the schema of "quadruped in general," with which I can refer to specific dogs.[17] Here, too, the "quadruped in general" is an odd creature, a useless shadow that disappears as soon as we try to pin it down.

It is quite unclear why Kant speaks of a "method of construction" here. If anything, what we have is a *process of exemplification*, a sort of diagrammatic version of general ideas: from a plate I get the diagram of circular objects; from a poodle plus a dash of imagination, that of an Alsatian. And that it is this that is clearly going on comes out in §59 of the *Critique of Judgment*, where Kant again says that empirical concepts, like plate or dog, are not schemata, but instances; that is to say, they are diagrams and not monograms. As we shall see, in the version given in the third *Critique*, all empirical concepts are rendered sensible by way of instances,[18] and abstract concepts such as "substance" and "cause" are mere rules for reflection. In this way, Kant weakened the role assigned to concepts, turning it into a merely epistemological function that is necessary not for experience, but for reflection on experience.

Nevertheless, in the *Critique of Pure Reason*, he will not make do with so little, because he claims that at least some concepts determine experience a priori. On the one hand, he offers some very general determinations of the schemata, of the sort envisaged in the austere interpretation.[19] These do not go beyond definitions of Substance, Cause, Reciprocal Action, Possibility, Actuality, and so on; to which it is added that they are forms of time. On the other hand, Kant gives indications like "*silhouette*," "plate," and "dog," which are aimed at explaining the passage from the very abstract principles to experience. The tension between these two levels can be felt throughout the chapter on the Schematism and is heightened by the fact that Kant makes a further reference to the imagination to motivate referring the abstract to the concrete. But he maintains that we know nothing about the imagination, just as we know nothing of the real workings of the Schematism.

What is the point here? The problem, in general, is that it does not seem hard to conceive of a movement from the pure concept of substance to the schema of that concept. But nor is it hard to think of the passage from the empirical concept of a dog to the schema of that concept, and hence to the dog. What is left unclear is how the first model holds for experience and how the second has something to do with the a priori and, above all, how the first is attached to the second. The moral is that the problem of the schematism is left open at precisely the point where it should be resolved.

How a schema works: A speculative hypothesis

That said, I would like to propose, on the basis of some remarks that Kant makes, a possible interpretation of the schematism that seeks to fill in the reference to the "forms of time." From this purely speculative point of view, I think that there are three elements called for to explain how the schema functions as a "method of construction." Of these three elements, two are not even mentioned by Kant himself, and the third appears in the text as an illustration; the elements in question are number, the operations, and line.

The trick is simple. To make concepts, or rather very thin features of concepts, homogeneous with their objects, we commonly make use of numbers: three potatoes, one hundred kilometers per hour, 36 percent of Italians, and so on. This works up to a certain point, precisely because the features in question are very impoverished relative to the object. Kant must have thought that by complicating these resources, he could arrive at a much denser description such that he could individuate concrete particulars.[20]

As regards *number*, Descartes and modern physicists transcribe nature in quantitative terms, thus putting percept and concept on a level. Roughly, what we have in Kant is the converse move, starting from the hypothesis that the physicists' work is the completion of a task performed spontaneously by our souls.

As to the *operations*, the categories supply purely intellectual syntheses that function like the basic arithmetic operations. We thus have $7 + 5 = 12$; $12 - 5 = 7$; $7 \times 5 = 35$; and $35 \div 7 = 5$. Except that at the level of the categories, while the operations are pretty straightforward for quantity and quality, they are rather different for relation,[21] and they are really difficult to conceive of for modality. In this way, once more, the only two pure principles that Kant commits himself to and that he really makes use of in his proofs of the transcendentalness of the categories turn out to be Substance and Cause. At this point, we have a passage from arithmetic to geometry, that is, from thought to extension.

This is where the *line* comes in. Kant offers an enlightening example to explain the difference between an image and a schema as method of construction when he cites the number 5, which can construct •••••. It is surely for simplicity's sake that Kant did not write that the number 5 can construct, say, €€€€€, @@@@@, or \$\$\$\$\$, but there is underlying his procedure the traditional idea that time is made up of instants that are set out in a linear trajectory (time's arrow), just as space is made up of points that generate lines, in a passage from the discrete to the continuous.[22] This is in every respect the conception that underlies the schematism. On five separate occasions Kant cites the same example of the schema to illustrate the possibility of representing time by means of a line,[23] as if to give phenomenological confirmation to the idea that arithmetic has a geometrical counterpart and time has a spatial counterpart.

The timeline

Kant's basic idea is this: we are producers of time, taken as a movement that arises in the "I" by the addition of units that are so many temporal instants. The units serve to make up a line in our imagination, which offers an external and figured representation of time.[24] In the world, things have outlines, or lines, as on a silhouette that constitute extended magnitudes.[25] When we see a thing, we also, and in that moment, think it, and the unity of the object corresponds to the unity of consciousness with respect to that object.[26]

It is worth adding that not one of the references to the line appears in the schematism: the first is in the Aesthetic, another three are in the Deduction, and the last is in the Principles. But I can see no other way to understand the claim that the schemata are the forms of time and methods of construction. Moreover, in the scattered references to the line, as in the Schematism, Kant makes further appeal to the imagination as what colors concepts and renders them homogeneous with percepts, and as what draws the line.

However that may be, in Kant's intention, the line illustrates three things. First, that time can become space, given that we represent it in the imagination as a line. Second, that the "I think" connects representations in just the way that we connect instants to draw the line that represents time, and in this way the "I think" also connects a single representation as an extended magnitude. And third, that the unity of consciousness arises out of this unity of the phenomena. Which was what Kant proposed to prove, so long as we are already convinced of the conclusion.

Why it doesn't work

If, by chance, someone were not convinced, our conjecture leaves at least four questions unresolved.

How does the line fold? That is, how do we get from geometrical forms to empirical concepts in general?

In what way does the line help us to refer to particular empirical concepts? Crawling babies, radiators, and dogs can all be identified in the same way, which echoes what we saw in Chapter 8 as the calamitous underdetermination of Substance as the endurance of something through time.

Who adds or subtracts the colors, and why are the colors exactly these? To say that, as an intuition that is not too sensible, time mediates between concepts and percepts seems no different from saying that a green window mediates between the air and a leaf because it is translucent like the air and green like the leaf.[27]

And, finally, much the same problems that we raised in Chapter 8 about mental images and representations in relation to the Thesis of the "I think" can be raised about the schemata: images resemble objects, but it is only resemblance.

All of these considerations may testify in favor of the greater adaptability of the schemata relative to things, because they are more abstract and more indeterminate. But the other side of the coin is the fact that it becomes hard to explain how they can give a thicker description of objects than numbers can. In the end, the only shapes that are identifiable would be silhouettes, and the only forms that would be constructible would be of the sort that we encounter in a child's "join-the-dots" puzzle or in the advertisement for Lagostina saucepans:

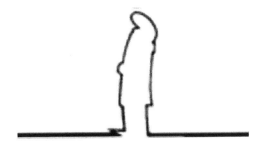

Figure 16. Lagostina man

Could it have worked?

Kant's solution seems to be parsimonious with its resources: from the psychological contingency that we have to conceive of time as a line, he reaches the technical possibility of applying the categories to experience. But it is extremely wasteful with the means put to work. For Kant has to invoke an unknown faculty to apply a coat of paint, in the figural synthesis, to the pure schemata supplied by the intellectual synthesis.[28] But Kant's problem was that of giving an explanation of why, through physics, mathematics fits experience so well, in such a way that the explanation would appear adequate, while, at least in those terms, it was really redundant.

Fourth Gadget: Principles

The principles of pure intellect are the upshot of the whole chain, the finished product. Once we have proved as a matter of law, in the Deduction, and as a matter of fact, in the Schematism, that the categories derived from the judgments apply to experience, we can draw up a list of the logical principles that, along with the Aesthetic, which is to say, space and time, determine our normal relation with the world. As we have seen, there are four families of principles: the axioms of intuition, the anticipations of perception, the analogies of experience, and the postulate of empirical thought in general.

The axioms of intuition and the anticipations of perception correspond to the categories of quantity and quality, respectively. They are essentially numerical principles. Thus, for Kant, my measuring the length of a table with a ruler, the heat of a body with a thermometer, or the intensity of color with a photometer are just natural extensions of functions that I unreflectively carry out with the senses.

The postulates of empirical thought in general, which correspond to the category of modality, define an experience as possible, actual, or necessary. Nevertheless, Kant was the first to stress that they are of primarily epistemological, rather than ontological, interest. Which is pretty clear in the case of the hundred thalers: only the actual exists; what is merely possible does not; and necessity seems redundant.

The analogies of experience correspond to the category of relation. These are Substance, endurance in time, Cause, sequence in time, and Reciprocal Action, in which causes cancel out, as in the balance of a house of cards. It is at this point that Kant performs his final escape act, namely the justification of the crucial principles of Substance and Cause, which he derives from the "I think" that, as we have seen, was the starting point of the whole contraption.

Afterword on reciprocal action

Given that we discussed the "I think," Substance, and Cause at length in the previous chapter, I would like to close the rundown of our camera's features with a word about the curious principle of Reciprocal Action. Kant takes it that in order to be able to look at our desk, we need what Einstein spent the whole of the second part of his life looking for in vain, namely a Theory of Everything. This would bring out not just causal relations but also the states of equilibrium in which action and reaction are equal and opposite, as in houses of cards, tables set for dinner, or bikes propped up against the wall.

It would be hard to find an instance of the confusion between ontology and epistemology spelled out so heroically. It is right to remember that the principle that Kant is appealing to is Newton's third law of motion, that to each action there corresponds an equal and opposite reaction. This may also be expressed as the principle that the reciprocal action between two bodies is always equal. But as we experience the world, it is easy to think that the absence of such a relation of dependence is the rule rather than the exception.[29] Does it seem as if the pencil is interacting with the table? And if you say that it does, are you sure that you are not exaggerating, that you are really describing your experience?

From phenomena to screwdrivers

The deduction as naturalization

The challenge to describe experience as accurately as possible suggests a final theme. We have reviewed the two epistemological theses and the five ontological ones and set out both the statics and the dynamics of the transcendental logic. It is now time to look at Kant's manner of proceeding and, in particular, at the invention of which he was proudest, namely the Transcendental Deduction. And we should bear in mind that where he uses the contemporary juridical term "deduction" to refer to the justification of a claim's legitimacy, what he is up to corresponds to what modern philosophical jargon would call "naturalization," by which is meant the articulation of cultural undertakings in terms of the natural resources they call on.

From another point of view, one might ask why Kant had to appeal to physics, which set in motion the clumsy mechanism of the deduction. But we already know the answer: because physics presented the only response then available to the skeptical consequence of empiricism. If he had had, for instance, Darwinian theory at his disposal, then it would have been enough to say that we are as we are because we evolved in a world that is as it is. Though a response of this sort might seem Panglossian in implicitly supposing that our world is the best of all possible,[1] there would have been no need for a transcendental deduction; some reference to motor skills and bodily schemes as results of natural selection would have done the trick.[2] Such schemes are hardly strong epistemology insofar as we share them with other animals, but they would have supplied a low-level account of our responses to stimuli from the external world in place of the dressed-up parade of constructive principles. And they would have left open the possibility of a background realism in place of a transcendentalism: the world has and imposes its laws, and living creatures adapt to them if and when they can.

But this was not obvious to Kant.[3] Nevertheless, over time, his outlook became ever more sophisticated. In the *Critique of Pure Reason*, we are faced with a strong deduction or naturalization in which the conceptual schemes and our perceptual apparatus make possible both scientific knowledge and natural experience. They do so by determining the *form* of the objects we encounter, which are, therefore, phenomena (things for us) and not things in themselves. In the two later *Critiques*, this setup undergoes a transformation, as we may briefly see.

The *Critique of Practical Reason*

In the *Critique of Practical Reason*, Kant makes a much weaker-sounding claim, which effectively sets the problem of the deduction aside. Putting faith rather than knowledge at center stage, Kant outlines a world in which the intellect not only does not lay down the law to nature, it is wholly cut off from it. This is the realm of reason, where that is understood not as the capacity to categorize sensibility, but rather as our capacity to set objectives for ourselves. If I want to be just, I do not apply the concept "justice" to a just percept, because no percept can be so. Rather, I pursue the idea of justice. I follow a certain path or cultivate what is essentially a form of inner life.

At least for Kant, we have gone beyond the sphere of ontology and entered that of metaphysics, understood as the transcendence of the sensible world. Hence the correspondence between physics and transcendental philosophy no longer holds and is no longer called for. The free causality with which we decide to behave morally appears as a matter of definition completely separate from the causality of nature, which always forms a necessary causal chain.

Another point should be stressed. The Dialectic in the *Critique of Pure Reason* looks ahead to the results of the *Critique of Practical Reason*. The Soul, God, and the World are ideas that are necessary for reason and are not concepts applied to experience. That they exist not only is neither proven nor disproven, but they cannot be, given that, by definition, an idea can never have an instance in spatio-temporal experience. What, then, is the point of hypothesizing them? Here, too, Kant makes a strong point: we have to think that Soul, God, and World exist because otherwise we would have no idea what to do in life. We would be more or less like plants that depend on light and need to be watered. But are we sure we are not plants? The great Baruch Spinoza (1632–1677) pointed out that if a stone could think, it might believe that it was free as it fell. But it is good to assume that we are free; otherwise all our institutions and all our vocabulary would have to be changed, and human life would turn out to be very different from what it seems.

This move from a matter of fact to a hypothesis already points toward the *Critique of Judgment*. And in doing so, it brings to the fore the tensions generated by this outlook's extreme idealization of moral life. On the one hand, Kant maintains that there exist only tables and chairs. On the other hand, he doesn't take account of the ways that the obligations arising from social objects are not made just by us and can be as "solid as trees and tables":[4] anyone who hasn't paid his or her telephone bill will get this point. In conclusion, Kant shows himself to be too sublime in ethics, which turns into an idea-hunt, precisely because he is too down-to-earth in ontology. Granted this much, however, the assumption that the phenomenal world is not determined by the "I," which is a true legislator only in morals, begins to take shape, albeit negatively.

The *Critique of Judgment*

In the *Critique of Practical Reason*, then, there is not a trace of naturalization because Kant is talking about a supersensible world that is ruled by the laws of liberty and not of nature, of the noumenon and not of the phenomenon. In the *Critique of Judgment*, on the other hand, we find a weak naturalization, in which Kant shows himself much more modern than he does in the strong version of the first *Critique*. The basic idea is that our categories do not determine the world, but merely explain it relative to ends. Which is very reasonable: there is a huge difference between saying that a screwdriver is not a thing in itself but just a phenomenon for us and remarking that a screwdriver does not have an end in itself but only *for us* who use it as a tool. The framework of the first *Critique* thus has been modified in three main respects.

Where judgments conferred a determining form prior to experience by way of the categories, now reflective judgment follows the opposite path. Now we begin with the given and search for the rule, which Kant takes to be purely subjective. It is we as rational subjects who find the laws in nature, instead of imposing them as objectively valid and binding on the phenomena, as in the first *Critique*.

Reflective judgments, in turn, are articulated into aesthetic and teleological. Once more, the former is purely epistemological insofar

as it concerns the relation between subject and object, rather than the
determination of an object. According to Kant's understanding, when I
say that I like something, I am not saying anything about anything that
belongs to the object as a property. The judgment is therefore subjective,
although in formulating it I presuppose that other subjects may agree
with me. It is worth noting that, in this context, Kant says that "the
beautiful pleases without concept,"[5] which is in clear tension with the
claim that "intuitions without concepts are blind."

The other specification of reflective judgments, namely teleological
judgment, is the active side of aesthetic judgment. If aesthetic judgment
responds to the question "Do I like it or not?," the teleological judgment
(from the Greek, *telos*, meaning end or purpose) answers the question
"What use is it, what is it for?."

This last move seems to be by far the most decisive, turning the
deduction from a determination of objects (strong thesis) into a recognition of ends (weak thesis). If I look at the cross section of an eye, Kant
observes,[6] I cannot understand what this ensemble of vitreous humor,
ciliary processes, and whatnot could be. But if I'm told that the eye is
made for seeing, then everything changes: the parts acquire meaning and
their relations become clear. Do we have an objective purposiveness here?
Despite it all, we do not. To a certain degree, the eye is made for seeing
and the heart is made to pump blood, much as bank notes are made for
making payments and the law about which side of the road to drive on
is made to reduce accidents. Such things are *made*, constructed, or stipu-
lated, not encountered as *given*. It is we, given the interests of humans,
and not those of the objects, who establish the purposes, in a process not
unlike that in which we decide that a tumor is an illness, where, from
the point of view of the objects, the cancerous cells have nothing "bad"
about them relative to the other cells of the organism.

To suppose that purposiveness is a feature of objects and not added
by observing and evaluating subjects would lead to the absurdity of supposing that lice were created to instill a sense of hygiene in people. It
may not be much, but it is certain that this is not how things are. There
is nothing wrong with noting that grass is good for cattle and that cattle
are useful to men. But it is quite unclear why men should exist at all,
especially when they go and set up shop in inhospitable place like New
Netherlands or Tierra del Fuego.[7] Kant is quite right to poke fun at the
optimism of the Leibnizians who were convinced that this is the best
of all possible worlds; as Voltaire's Candide comments, "What must the
worst be like?"; but, in effect, he has to review the whole framework of

the *Critique of Pure Reason*. The whole business of imposing rational ends, which I have expressed in terms of the naturalization of physics, now becomes an *epistemological* and not an ontological endeavor. It concerns the dispositions of subjects and not the characteristics of objects.

We may take up again an example mentioned at the beginning of this chapter to show this. When he is criticizing the Leibnizians for postulating objective purposes in nature, Kant takes the same line that he does when he attacks their claim to know things in themselves, noumena, rather than things as they appear to us, phenomena. But, as we saw in Chapter 6, it is very hard to hold that *everything* is phenomenon; that the screwdriver, the screw, and the pieces of the DIY bookcase I am struggling with are phenomena and not things in themselves. After all, they display a proud autonomy, even a gritty recalcitrance, in the face of my purposes. On the other hand, it seems reasonable to say that using a screwdriver to screw in a screw that will, if I am lucky, hold the bookcase together forms part of a system of ends that exists for me but not for a squirrel. For the squirrel is unable to use the screwdriver and has no use for a bookcase. Yet some of the physical properties of the object, such as its solidity, hold good equally for me and for the squirrel.

In short, the former account is that of the *Critique of Pure Reason*, and the latter that of the *Critique of Judgment*. Between the two, Kant recognized that the "for us" is not a feature of *every* object, but just of those peculiar objects that are *tools* or *instruments*, whether screwdrivers, bathtubs, airplanes, or books. And the same holds of *institutions*—try putting a beaver in a post office, and you'll grasp that it is a very different thing for him from what it is for us—and of *organized systems*, whether nature or the human body, viewed from the point of view of human interests. In its drastic version, then, the Copernican revolution was over after a mere nine years of life. Goodbye, Kant?

Reckoning with the revolution

A spectre is haunting Europe

We might not say so. After initial resistance, Kant did achieve one thing: becoming by far the thinker who exercised most influence, direct and indirect, on philosophy for two centuries, the nineteenth and the twentieth. The Copernican revolution has opened up many routes, and above all, it has closed off not a few. It put on the defensive the sort of more or less naive realism that had dominated philosophy since Aristotle and that had been dealt a severe—perhaps too severe—blow by Descartes. It has promised work for philosophers and has assured them an income: as professionals of conceptual schemes, they have known what to do, and if they become psychologists, they have been able to make themselves specialists in perceptual systems. This was the right thing to do. From then on, despite widespread but scattered resistance, modern philosophy has been in very large measure a series of footnotes to Kant, just as ancient philosophy was a gloss on Plato.

This can easily be shown.[1] The Idealisms and anti-Idealisms, the Rationalisms and Irrationalisms of the last two centuries are quite unintelligible without Kant's contribution. All of these views derive ultimately from the shift in the center of gravity from objects to the subjects that know them. And it would be no exaggeration to say that 80 percent of the philosophies of the nineteenth and twentieth centuries are indebted, if not to the details of Kantian philosophy, then at least to the Copernican revolution.

Kantianism is no longer just a school of thought: it is an entire style of thinking whose effects spread far beyond its direct influences. Even the linguistic turn that is characteristic of a major phase of the twentieth century,[2] with the idea that philosophical problems can be resolved or dissolved by analyzing the language we speak, would be unimaginable without Kant, for language is given the transcendental role that the categories had for Kant. Not to mention that anthropology, psychology, the human sciences in general, and even cognitive science find their basic drive in the Kantian notion that, if you want to understand the world, you must first understand humans, their minds, and their senses. In this way, all the basic ideas that have rejuvenated philosophy in the last two hundred years, including those that seem to want to break with traditional philosophy or indeed with philosophy tout court, all come from Kant.

Honor where it is due. The trouble is that, along with his solutions, Kant left so many new problems, and left so many of them unresolved. Let us try to sum them up by reviewing the three *Critiques* a last time.

Matrix

Let us begin with the outstanding problem of the ontology of the first *Critique*. From the vantage point of the Copernican revolution, everything is real, but is so within our conceptual schemes and relative to our perceptual apparatus. Though Kant would never have admitted it, this meant that, even if we were brains in vats of organic liquid stimulated electrically by a mad scientist, the objectivity of our knowledge would not be altered one jot.[3] Kant calls this "empirical realism," which, in his view, does not exclude the transcendental idealism that says that everything depends on our conceptual schemes. There are at least two advantages to this. One is the defeat of skepticism by way of a thesis that touches on and courts skepticism, but that makes the world safe and the object of rational enquiry. The other is a division of labor, in which scientists busy themselves with the way the world is and philosophers with the way we know it.

At first glance, Kant's world is the world of *Matrix*: nothing is really real; everything is just an appearance that strikes our senses.[4] And this is indeed how Kant was understood by many of his contemporaries and successors: performing the Copernican revolution is just a change of colored glasses: sometimes the world looks red and sometimes it looks blue. In fact, the game is rather more sensible and sophisticated. The world is out there independently of what we perceive, think, and know of it. We humans see it in one way that is the same for everybody. Other beings see it in a different way or perhaps do not see it at all. But no one creates and no one invents. In other words, our world is the same as a bat's,[5] except that we see things where they echolocate them. The dominant reading of Kant was one according to which the world is constructed by the "I"; this went beyond his intentions, but is after all authorized by his philosophy.[6] Like all great revolutions, Kant's did not happen without bloodshed, for at least three reasons.

First, if the realm of the knowable is limited to what is in space and time, then metaphysics becomes a province of physics. As a result, there comes into being a very wide range of things that cannot be seen and cannot be touched and that end up being equivalent: God, the origin of the world, the walk I took yesterday, and the requirement to fasten my safety belt. Kant had huge respect for the things that are neither in Heaven nor on Earth and even held that they were the most important things for metaphysics. Except that he had concluded that they could not be known and that, at the end of the day, it was better thus. For instance, if we saw God as we see tables and chairs, we would not act out of morality but out of hope or fear.[7] Suppose this holds for God and for the immortality of the soul, where the argument seems cogent. But one does not see the requirement not to break the speed limit, either: one sees the signs and, sometimes, the fines; does this mean it doesn't exist or that it is at best a noumenon? We had to wait for a century before this prejudice in favor of the merely actual would be taken to task[8] and the much—indeed, too much—that Kant had excluded would be reinstated in an ontology that would have room for Madame Bovary and Sherlock Holmes, the number five, and the equilateral triangle, as well as the immense range of laws, obligations, and norms that make up our social life and that constitute a "huge, invisible ontology" to which Kant never gave due attention.[9]

Second, if what we know depends on what we are like, then philosophy becomes an offshoot of psychology. The subtly anti-Kantian battle that philosophy has fought over the last two hundred years to distinguish a subject's psychological acts from their objective content—my thinking about a triangle from the triangle I am thinking about—has been a reaction, at first timid and then ever more blatant, to this conception.[10]

Third, and perhaps most importantly, despite Kant's best intentions, the distinction between "being" and "knowing," between objective and subjective, is obliterated. Berkeley[11] queried whether a tree falling in a forest without observers really made a sound and thus opened the way to the sort of dogmatic idealism in which, in the *Critique of Pure Reason*, Kant refuses to recognize a real enemy.[12] Yet Kant maintains something that is, at least in appearance, less committal, but that leaves him with the same result. What is not known may as well not exist: it is a noumenon, a mere shot in the dark. But because knowledge is still something that happens in a subject, for all that it is a transcendental subject, the distinction between subjective and objective boils down to a pious hope.

What became of Kant is after all what became of another Prussian, the Baron Münchhausen: it must be admitted that ensuring a stable and objective world by referring everything to the subject is no easier than getting oneself out of a mud pool by pulling oneself up by the scruff of the neck. We can see this at work in three examples in increasing order of seriousness insofar as they call into question, first, the "phenomenon" as distinct from the "thing in itself"; second, the distinction between the subjective and the objective; and, finally, the mere possibility of morality, which for Kant is the underlying objective of any philosophy worthy of the name.

First, the things we know are phenomena: the red is not in the rose. But where, then, as we asked in Chapter 6, is the red? In our heads? If so, why is it red and not another color?

Second, and getting to the point, what difference is there between perceiving objectively and subjectively? Kant offers an example that has become famous.[13] I can look at a house from the foundation up to the roof or from the roof down to the foundation; either way, the order is subjective, which I can change if I want to. But if I see a boat floating down a river, we have an objective perception, because I cannot reverse the order at will: the boat is down here, and I cannot make it return higher up just by moving my head. Now, the distinction between subjective and objective here seems to be presupposed just at the point at which we seem to have found a criterion for distinguishing the two. And it falls apart as soon as we try to apply it to a slightly more complicated case.[14] Suppose we are approaching a coast in a boat; how do Kantian principles help to show that it is we who are doing the approaching and not the coast that is coming toward us?[15]

Third, morality. Perhaps Kant would have replied that these issues are secondary and that what matters is not so much what we can know as what we can hope for and what we ought to do. All of these abstract doubts would evaporate if we had to take a moral decision. For Kant, everything that went missing in the world of knowledge gathering, where things become phenomena and what we don't touch doesn't exist, is recovered in full in the moral world, where we are masters of our own intentions. Very well, but what intentions would these be if there were no external world, if we were unable to distinguish euphoria from happiness, depression from unhappiness, and having friends from thinking we have some?

Kant and Talleyrand

Perhaps this is the most serious problem, especially given the importance that Kant rightly attributed to morality. The conclusion of the *Critique of Practical Reason* is famous, even notorious, for saying that "two things fill the mind with ever new and increasing admiration and awe: the starry heavens above and the moral law within." In the former, we are slaves of causality; in the latter, we are masters of our own freedom. Yet there is a non-negligible problem with this. We all see the starry heavens, but we don't all see the moral law, and, for all that Kant says about it, it may not even exist. Or, rather, it really doesn't exist, given that, as we have seen, it has no place in the realm of phenomena and is, for precisely that reason, moral. In short, it's the thought that counts. Which is a terrible principle when it comes to gift making and is no less problematic in ethics: someone who thinks they are doing good may nevertheless wreak havoc yet be a moral hero for Kant.

Charles Maurice de Talleyrand Périgord (1754–1838), a bishop and minister of great staying power serving under Louis XVI, Napoleon, and Louis XVIII, was very shrewd about ethics, including Kantian ethics, as can be seen from the remark attributed to him that principles are a splendid thing because they don't commit anyone to anything. So it is always fine to raise points of principle, and it is very useful to talk in general, adopting compelling but vague maxims. In the same years, Kant himself behaved (in theory) exactly like Talleyrand and wrote that we ought to act as though the maxim of our actions were to become by our will a universal law of nature.[16] As we have seen, Kant claims that, in its pure form, morality is played out in a fully intelligible world, where space and time have no role, where our bodies and the fact that we are objects as well as subjects is at most a source of minor friction, like the resistance of the air that, as Kant himself says, allows the dove to fly. Air resistance and drag are, thus, the merest accidents.

Why should we not think that it is exactly the other way around? Let us try a little thought experiment. If just a few of the features of our bodies and of the physical world were different, then the whole of our morality would be different. If we could move our bodies from place to place as easily as we can travel in thought, probably none of our current values would hold. If we lived for only ten seconds, our values would be entirely different, or perhaps we would have none. And likewise if we were immortal.

What's more, if we set ourselves to look for moral purity in the marketplace with a lantern, the inevitable result would be that everything would be appalling and corrupt. If only intentions count and we have no authentic certainty about the existence of the external world, then someone who has merely been tempted by the idea of a crime would be as bad as someone who has actually committed it.[17] Bereft of pity because obsessed by principles, Kantian morality's ferocity has been stressed in works from the novella *Michael Kohlhaas* (1810) by Heinrich von Kleist (1777–1811) to Lars von Trier's film *Dogville* (2003). Friedrich Schiller (1759–1805) clearly saw the absurdity in the idea that what is moral is only what is contrary to inclination, and hence that it is immoral to help family and friends. The inapplicability of a purely formalistic morality was drawn out in the twentieth century.[18] And the impossibility of a fleshless ethics, not to mention the problematic character of the notion of "disinterestedness," infects the third *Critique* with difficulties.

An Iroquois in Paris

Indeed, also in the matter of the simple analysis of aesthetic pleasure, it is not hard to find troubles for Kant's argument, which defines that sort of pleasure as *disinterested*, without ever being explicit about the sort of disinterestedness that is in question. But if it is not a pleasure, what pleasure is it? Already in ethics, the theoretical problem is not minor. And in aesthetics it becomes enormous: How can we have a taste for something that, in its very essence, demands that it not be tasted? Kant's solution is to say that the taste involved in aesthetic experience is not for something edible. This is another sense in which *Carmina non dant panem* ("Songs do not give bread"). Conversely, eating something or someone up, even if only with one's eyes, is an infallible sign of interest.

Let us take a case of this. The whole of the *Critique of Judgment*, in which Kant asserts and defends the axiom of disinterested pleasure, is crisscrossed with counterexamples from the realm of eating. The emblematic case of this is the Sachem of the Iroquois, who, of all the wonders of Paris, appreciated only the taverns or eating houses (according to the preferred translation). He is a barbarian incapable of disinterested pleasure, of which the proof is that the only things he likes are those he can eat.

This is not the only instance. Let us take the art of gardening, which in Kant's day was one of the fine arts, a status to which it is returning today. Now, flowers have colors and aromas, and Kant concludes that the authentically aesthetic experience lies in the form of the flower or the garden and not in the matter. Why? If the case of the Sachem is anything to go by, it is because we can eat matter if we suppose that there are fruit trees, and, in any case, you can make roses into a salad. But form cannot be eaten; hence it is disinterested aesthetic pleasure.

Again, the sublime, which is for Kant the outsized version of beauty either in dimensions, as in a colossal object, or in power, as in an earthquake or a storm at sea. Kant calls the former sort "mathematical sublime" because it is a matter of size, and the latter is the "dynamic sublime" as involving power. But even here, pleasure in an earthquake, or a storm can only be experienced by a spectator and not by an agent. Why? Obviously because, otherwise, we would be too interested in not being *swallowed* by earth or the sea.

Last example. Kant is certainly not alone in thinking of the human body as the form par excellence of beauty. Here, too, the reason may be connected with nutrition. In the normal way of things, men are not to be eaten, nor are women. But a pig is, and nothing is wasted. Indeed, there are a great many paintings of pigs and even a few statues. Chris Noonan's 1995 film *Babe* makes a piglet aesthetically, and not gastronomically, appealing purely by humanizing it. And still lifes depicting fruit and sometimes fish and game are regarded as constituting a minor genre relative to human portraiture. But in any case, they are not edible, though they might torment a hungry viewer. As in the earlier cases, here, too, the underlying suspicion of materialness and the favor shown toward universalizable form produce insurmountable difficulties for Kantian philosophy.

From Kant to Kafka

Have there been too many victims of the glorious revolution? That is not the point. Kant fought, if anything, too successfully against common sense, against a naive view of things, against an immediate relation with the world. And he did so not with the inconclusiveness of a skeptic, but with the constructive desire of an honest philosopher who was also one of the great figures of human thought: he is one of the few men to whom this description can be applied without irony. The path that he pointed out has often turned out to be a shortcut, but it was also the only one that metaphysics could take to get out of the slough in which it found itself. The return of realism two hundred years after the Kantian turn is not, then, the result of a tedious pendulum swing, but it is likely to be a sign that that turn has been fully assimilated. A naive view of the world is possible and even necessary, but the naiveté is not given and must be earned. How?

In the nineteenth century, the reactions against Kantianism did
not come either from the positivist heirs of empiricism or from the his-
toricist heirs of idealism and rationalism, but from a rather unexpected
quarter.[19] It may be worthwhile to close our brief story with an account
of this movement, if only because we can use it, along with the law of
anniversaries that dictated the writing of this book, to ponder the law of
the transmigration of souls. The Bohemian priest Bernhard Bolzano died
in 1848, the very year that Gottlob Frege was born. Frege would die in
1925, but he unconsciously took over Bolzano's legacy, probably without
ever having read his writings. Bolzano's pupil, Franz Příhonský, who was
himself also a priest in Prague, died in 1859, the year of the battle of
Solferino, when Alexius Meinong, another hero of Austro-Hungarian
anti-Kantianism, was only six years only.

What holds these harbingers and avatars together? A fierce anti-
Kantianism that was common to the climate of Austrian Catholicism;
Frege is the odd man out here as a northern German and a Protestant.
This attitude had already been expressed by Bolzano,[20] and, as we noted
at the outset, the message was carried forward by Příhonský.[21] What was
the basic error of Kantianism? Precisely the Copernican revolution, which
had made the world into a creation of an "I" that had usurped the place
of God. This could not please Catholic priests, but Bolzano and Příhonský
did not merely remonstrate. They set themselves to restoring a world that
exists independently of any "I" that may think about it.

The pillar that brings the whole edifice crashing down is their critique of the notion of "pure sensible intuition." There simply are no intuitions of this sort. Sensible intuitions have just one object; they make up
single representations; otherwise they would be mixed with concepts and
cease to be intuitions. When Kant wrote of "pure sensible intuitions," of
"pure forms of intuition" (space and time), or again of "the manifold of
intuition" synthesized by the "I," he was referring to incoherent objects
that are neither in the Heaven of concepts nor on the Earth of intuitions. Consequently, it is not the case that intuitions without concepts
are blind: they see perfectly well, in just the sense that I see this table in
this instant. If I then want to add the concept "table," that is an entirely
different question.

What really matters to Bolzano and Příhonský is thought. In their
view, it is absurd to connect it with the activity of a subject, of an "I
think." Insofar as it is a priori, necessity has its home in concepts, not
in the "I." And this is the point of departure both for Meinong's theory
of objects,[22] which has essentially been understood as a theory of non-

existent objects, and for Frege's logic,[23] in which the decisive distinction is between thought as an objective and shared content and thoughts as the psychological acts of individuals that refer to that content.

Who was right? Certainly the Austrian Catholics grasp an important point: reality cannot be reduced to what is accessible to a subject placed in space and time, lest the world be so impoverished as to be in the end virtually unmanageable.[24] On the other hand, however, by affirming the objective reality of thought, their world admits roundsquares and Pegasus. As a result, they find themselves in even worse difficulties than the Leibnizians in distinguishing between logic and ontology, between mere thought and what enters into our sensible experience. Understood this way, they were probably both wrong: Kant allows too few real things; the Austrians too many, including the hundred ideal thalers.

Another son of the Habsburg empire, the Moravian Edmund Husserl, pointed out a middle way:[26] necessity, which is of such importance in philosophy, is not to be found only in the propositions of logic, as the defenders of the conceptual a priori hold, or in the discoveries of physics, as Kant believed, but in the world and its laws. There can be no color without extension, no musical note without duration: Why should such laws be placed in the subject, when they apply so well to objects? The necessity that Kant saw in the categories applied to experience, and that Bolzano and his followers placed in the slightly Platonic world of concepts, Husserl finds in experience itself. Reason can give itself as much work as it likes: the objects remain there, as impassive and solid as trees and houses, even when they are laws and norms, and even when they are that rather queer sort of object that is a subject. Another faithful servant of the Austro-Hungarian empire, Franz Kafka, pointed out this necessity: "We are like tree trunks in the snow. In appearance they lie sleekly and a little push should be enough to set them rolling. No, it can't be done, for they are firmly wedded to the ground."[26]

Notes

Introduction

1. We have no intention of offering an introduction to Kant or to the *Critique of Pure Reason*, of which there are many available. Those for an Italian readership would include R. Ciafardone, *La Critica della ragion pura. Introduzione alla lettura* (Rome: La Nuova Italia Scientifica, 1996); A. Guerra, *Introduzione a Kant*. 12th ed. (Rome-Bari: Laterza, 1999); S. Marcucci, *Guida alla lettura della Critica della ragion pura di Kant* (Rome-Bari: Laterza, 1997); G. Riconda, *Invito al pensiero di Kant* (Milan: Mursia, 1987). Also translated into Italian is the useful guide offered by O. Höffe, *Immanuel Kant* (Munich: C. H. Beck, 1983). English translation by M. Farrier (Albany: SUNY Press, 1994).

2. As the Kantian or Kantophile Bartolomeo Vanzetti wrote to his sister Luigina on December 8, 1926, "Through suffering, misfortune and defeat, following in the footsteps of the ancient Stoic philosophy and of the only heroic school of modern philosophy, I have learnt to overcome fear and pain, I have learnt to be happy." The original Italian is in *Il caso Sacco e Vanzetti. Lettere ai familiari*, ed. C. Pillon and V. Vanzetti (Rome, 1971, pp. 167–8), this letter is not included in *The Letters of Sacco and Vanzetti*, ed. Marion D. Frankfurter et al. (Harmondsworth: Penguin, 1997).

3. F. Příhonský, *Neuer Anti-Kant* (1850), critical edition by E. Morscher and Christian Thiel (Sankt Augustin: Academia Verlag, 2003) (Beiträge zur Bolzano-Forschung, vol. 9).

4. The first was in fact the *Anti-Kant* of the Jesuit Benedikt Stattler (1728–1797), which appeared in two volumes in 1788.

Chapter 1

1. "A" and "B" refer to the pagination of the first and second editions (1781 and 1787, respectively) of the *Critique of Pure Reason*. Except where noted, English translations follow the classic text of Norman Kemp Smith (London: Macmillan, 1929). The abbreviation "Ak" refers to the standard critical edition of Kant's writings, *Kant's gesammelte Schriften hg. v. der Königlich Preussischen Aka-*

demie der Wissenschaften (Berlin-Leipzig 1900–) (subsequently *Deutsche Akademie der Wissenschaften* [Berlin: de Gruyter, 1967–]). (Translator's note: where possible, we have supplied references to English versions of the works cited; where reference is made to works, especially in German, of which no English exists, the original is indicated, omitting the Italian bibliographic data; in a few instances, integrations of obvious English sources have been added.)

2. L. E. Borowski, R. B. Jachmann, and E. A. C. Wasianski, *Immanuel Kant. Sein Leben in Darstellungen von Zeitgenossen* (1804) (Berlin: Deutsche Bibliothek, 1912). On his illness, see Thomas de Quincey, *The Last Days of Immanuel Kant* (London, 1827).

3. B xvi–xviii.

4. I. Kant, *Critique of Judgment* (1790), §49 (Ak V, pp. 315–16).

5. A 51/B 75.

6. Nevertheless, the Sun King didn't fall into the trap; as we well know, Napoleon did fall into it when he invaded Egypt in 1798. A good English account of Leibniz's unification efforts is G. T. Jordan, *The Reunion of the Churches. A Study of G.W. Leibniz and his Great Attempt* (London, 1927).

7. P. Rossi, *Clavis universalis: arti della memoria e logica combinatoria da Lullo a Leibniz* (Milan: Ricciardi, 1960); 2nd ed. (Bologna: Il Mulino, 1983); see also F. A. Yates, *The Art of Memory* (London, 1966); I. Hacking, *The Emergence of Probability* (Cambridge: Cambridge University Press, 1975).

8. G. W. Leibniz, *Theodicy*, 1710, II, §414 (there appears to be no complete English translation of this work, which appears in vol. VI of Gerhardt's edition of the *Philosophische Schriften* (7 vols.) (Berlin, 1875–1890). In this climate, Cyrano de Bergerac—who, however strange it may seem, was a real person and a philosopher to boot—set himself to writing books that refer to possible worlds so as to relativize ours (*The States and Empires of the Moon*, 1657, and *The States and Empires of the Sun*, 1662, French text of both in *Libertins du XVIIe siècle*, ed. J. Prévot [Paris: Pléiade, 1998]). Literary histories count these tales as the first instances of science fiction.

9. J.-L. Borges, *Labyrinths*, selected and trans. D. A. Yates et al. (Harmondsworth: Penguin, 1970).

10. So that our world is just one of the infinitely many possible, though for the incurably optimistic Leibniz, it is the best.

11. "This much is already known: for every sensible line of straightforward statement, there are leagues of senseless cacophonies, verbal jumbles and incoherences" (trans. cit., p. 80). In another story, *Tlön, Uqbar, Orbis Tertius* (in *Labyrinths*, cit., pp. 27–43) Borges suggests other untoward consequences of a Leibnizian metaphysic. What he imagines is that, by a typographical oddity, a copy of the *Anglo-American Cyclopaedia* contains articles on nonexistent persons and worlds in which the reader believes, because of his faith in encyclopedias, finding nothing implausible in what is recounted. The question is: Does he know more or less than anyone else?

12. G. Tonally, *Da Leibniz a Kant. Saggi sul pensiero del Settecento*, edited by C. Cesa (Naples: Prismi, 1987).

13. A. Ferrarin, "Construction and Mathematical Schematism. Kant on the Exhibition of a Concept in Intuition," *Kant-Studien*, 86, 1995: 131–74.

14. D. R. Lachterman, *The Ethics of Geometry. A Genealogy of Modernity* (New York: Routledge, 1989).

15. A 712ff./B 740ff.

16. For Leibnizians, sensations are in general either obscure or clear, but they are not distinct, where thoughts can be clear and distinct. In the few, but possible, cases in which a sensation becomes also distinct (if I look at a triangle and think that it has three sides), then, for Leibnizians, it counts as a concept.

17. For instance, what is the exact extension of the concept "telephone"? If, by attaching my computer to a modem, I can make a call, why shouldn't the computer fall into the class of telephones?

18. Perhaps the limits of the word "freedom" suffice to show that someone who replies to the question "Are you free this evening?" by saying, "No, I'm the slave of blind destiny" would not be answering straight. But we don't know much more than that.

19. I. Kant, *Prolegomena to any future metaphysics that will be able to present itself as a science* (1783), ed. and trans. P. Gray-Lucas (Manchester: Manchester University Press, 1953), Preamble, p. 9 (Ak IV, p. 260).

20. J. Locke, *Essay concerning Human Understanding* (1689), ed. P. H. Nidditch (Oxford: Oxford University Press, 1975), Book II, chap. xxii.

21. D. Hume, *Treatise of Human Nature* (1739–1740), ed. P. H. Nidditch (Oxford: Oxford University Press, 1978), Book I, Part ii, §2.

22. Ibid., Book I, Part iv, §6. Libro I.

23. G. Berkeley, *Essay Towards a New Theory of Vision* (1709), in *The Works of George Berkeley* (9 vols.), ed. A. A. Luce and T. E. Jessop (London: Nelson, 1948–1957), §3.

24. The postmodernists of the end of the twentieth century were not in the least empiricists but were rather fervent rationalists; all the same, they too ran into the difficulties that arise from the rejection of metaphysics. For instance, if there is no reality external to and separate from our concepts, what sense does it make to speak of "knowledge"?

25. For more on this point, see Chapter 9.

26. The person in question was Sir Francis Galton (1822–1911), geographer, meteorologist, tropical explorer, founder of differential psychology, the first to use fingerprints for identification, pioneer statistician, and distant relation of Charles Darwin.

27. "Funes the Memorious," in *Labyrinths*, cit., pp. 87–95.

28. T. Reid, *Inquiry into the Human Mind on the Principles of Common Sense* (1764), in *Inquiry and Essays*, ed. R. E. Beanblossom and K. Lehrer (Indianapolis: Bobbs-Merrill, 1983).

29. From Hegel onward. Cf. G. W. F. Hegel, "Glauben und Wissen" (1802), ed. G. Lasson (Leipzig, 1928).

30. For example, H. J. Paton, *Kant's Metaphysics of Experience* (New York: The Humanities Press, 1965).

31. I. Kant, *Dreams of a Spirit-seer Elucidated by Dreams of Metaphysics* (1766), trans. E. F. Goerwitz (1900), ed. F. Sewall (Bristol: Thoemmes, 1992) (Ak II, pp. 315–68).

32. R. Casati, "Torri gemelle. Un evento o due?," *Il Sole 24 ore*, October 13, 2002.

33. E. Bencivenga, *La rivoluzione copernicana di Kant* (Milan: Mondadori, 2000).

34. As he asserts in the preface to the *Critique of Judgment*.

35. B xliii.

36. J. L. Austin, *Sense and Sensibilia*, ed. G. J. Warnock (Oxford: Oxford University Press, 1962), p. 2.

37. See I. Kant, *Anthropology from a Pragmatic Viewpoint*, ed. H. H. Rudnick, trans. V. L. Dowell (Carbondale: Southern Illinois University Press, 1996).

38. For argumentation on the point, I may be forgiven for referring to my *Estetica razionale* (Milan: Raffaello Cortina, 1997).

Chapter 2

1. Throughout the nineteenth century and into the twentieth, Kant scholarship racked its brains to explain why so intelligent a man should have written so chaotic a book. The almost unanimous verdict was that, after working at it for ten years, Kant could put up with it no longer and assembled as well as he could the snippets of manuscript. This hypothesis, which might be called the "cobbling-together theory," is confirmed by the unequal distribution of the book's parts.

2. Likewise, the Analytic is made up of two parts: the Analytic of Concepts and the Analytic of Principles. As we shall see in Chapter 9, however, these constitute a unitary process, which it is well to handle as such.

3. P. F. Strawson, *The Bounds of Sense: An Essay on Kant's* Critique of Pure Reason (London: Methuen, 1966), p. 24.

4. A 22/B 37.

5. A 30/B 46.

6. A 182/B 224.

7. A 189/B 232.

8. B 131.

9. A 51/B 75.

10. More modestly, Kant would say that we "know" only what exists in space and time. But, in Kant's view, what exists in space and time is just what is real, the rest being merely possible. For this reason, it is not unfair to cut to the chase and admit that, for Kant (and for the rest of us, as a matter of com-

mon sense), "to exist" has as its focal sense "to be in space and time." See the reflections on "possible," "necessary," and "real" in the Analogy of Experience, A 218ff./B 266ff., to which we return in Chapter 9. See also the discussion of the hundred thalers in Chapter 4.

11. A 20/B 34, departing slightly from Kemp Smith.

12. In this, he differs from Descartes, for whom what is discovered by the maneuver known as the *cogito* is a substance in itself, perfectly transparent to itself even if contentless.

Chapter 3

1. As the Italian poet Giosuè Carducci put it, "Immanuel Kant decapitated God/ Maximilien Robespierre the King."

2. A. G. Baumgarten, *Metaphysica* (1757, which is the edition used by Kant, though the first is dated 1739), anastatic reprint (Hildesheim: Georg Olms, 1982).

3. To be precise, in 1606, in the subtitle of a book by Jacob Lorhard, prior of the monastery at St. Gall in Switzerland, *Ogdoas Scholastica*, Sangalli, apud Georgium Strave.

4. The trend today is to regard ontology as a doctrine about objects in general and metaphysics as a specification of what these objects are, but this is obviously not Kant's usage. For a theoretical account of the question, see K. Mulligan, "Métaphysique et ontologie," in P. Engel (ed.), *Précis de philosophie analytique* (Paris: Puf, 2000); A. C. Varzi, "Ontologia e metafisica," in F. D'Agostini and N. Vassallo (eds.), *Storia della filosofia analitica* (Turin: Einaudi, 2002), pp. 157–93; E. Berti, "Ontologia o metafisica? Un punto di vista aristotelico," in C. Bianchi and A. Bottani (eds.), *Significato e ontologia* (Milan: Angeli, 2003), pp. 25–38. For a historical account, see. J.-F. Courtine, "Ontologie ou Métaphysique?," *Giornale di Metafisica* (1985), pp. 3–24; and J. École, "Une étape de l'histoire de la métaphysique: l'apparition de l'Ontologie comme discipline séparée," his (ed.), *Autour de la philosophie Wolffienne* (Hildesheim: Georg Olms, 2001), pp. 95–116.

5. B XV.

6. I. Kant, *Dreams of a Spirit-seer* (1766), cit., Part I, chap. 3 (Ak II, p. 342).

7. A 247/B 303.

8. H.-J. De Vleeschauwer, *The Development of Kantian Thought: The History of a Doctrine* (1939), trans. A. R. C. Duncan (London: Thomas Nelson, 1962).

9. F. Suárez, *Metaphysical Disputations* (1597), anastatic reprint (2 vols., 25 and 26 of *Opera Omnia*, 1856–1878) (Hildesheim: Georg Olms, 1965); translated only in parts into English: V: *Suárez on Individuation*, trans. J. J. E. Gracia (Milwaukee: Marquette University Press, 1982); VI: *On Formal and Universal Unity*, trans. J. F. Ross (Milwaukee: Marquette University Press, 1964); VII: *On the Various Kinds of Distinctions*, trans. C. Vollert (Milwaukee: Marquette

University Press, 1947); X, XI, and parts of XXII: *The Metaphysics of Good and Evil*, trans. J. J. E. Gracia and G. Davis (Munich: Philosophia, 1989); XVII, XVIII, and XIX: *On Efficient Causality*, trans. A. J. Freddoso (New Haven, CT: Yale University Press, 1994); and XXI: *On the Essence of Finite Being*, trans. N. J. Wells (Milwaukee: Marquette University Press, 1983). For a reconstruction of the formation of metaphysics, see J.-F. Courtine, *Suárez et le système de la métaphysique* (Paris: Presses Universitaires de Frances, 1990).

10. Christian Wolff, *Philosophia prima, sive ontologia, methodo scientifica pertractata, qua omnis cogitationis humanae principia continetur*, 1729, reprinted from the second edition of 1736 under the supervision of J. Ecole, *Gesammelte Werke*, Latin Series, II, 3 (Hildesheim: Georg Olms, 1962).

11. I. Kant, *Metaphysik L_2*, Ak XXVIII.2, p. 541.

12. M. Heidegger, *Kant and the Problem of Metaphysics* (1929), trans. R. Taft (Bloomington: Indiana University Press, 1990).

13. N. Hinske, "Die historischen Vorlagen der Kantischen Transzendentalphilosophie," *Archiv für Begriffsgeschichte*, XII (1968), pp. 86–113.

14. P. Kobau, *Essere qualcosa. Ontologia e psicologia in Wolff* (Turin: Trauben, 2004).

15. I. Kant, *Metaphysik L_2*, Ak XXVIII.2, 1, p. 543.

16. Aristotle, *Categories*, 1b 25–2a 10: *Substance* ("man," "horse"); *Quantity* ("two cubits long," "three cubits long"); *Quality* ("white," "grammatical"); *Relation* ("double," "greater"); *Place* ("in the Lyceum," "in the square"); *Time* ("yesterday," "last year"); *Condition* ("is lying," "is sitting"); *Possession* ("is wearing shoes," "is armed"); *Action* ("cuts," "burns"); *Undergoing* ("is cut," "is burnt").

17. See Chapter 9.

18. For a brief account of Kant's thought that pays due attention to the eighteenth-century context, see R. Ciafardone, *La Critica della ragion pura. Introduzione alla lettura*, cit.

19. A. G. Baumgarten, *Aesthetica* (1750), anastatic reprint (Hildesheim: Georg Olms, 1986) = *Theoretische Ästhetik* (1750–1758), trans. H. Schweizer (Hamburg: Felix Meiner Verlag, 1983) (though frequently referred to by literary critics not known for their knowledge of Latin and German, there appears to be no English version of this work). Despite Baumgarten's broad definition of aesthetics, Kant sets his face against the entire Leibnizian scheme, which posited a continuity between sensibility and intellect. Suffice it to say that the initial aim of the *Critique of Pure Reason*—as we can see from the title, *The Limits of Sensibility and of Intellect*, that Kant gave to the very first drafts of the work—was precisely to mark a conceptual distinction between feeling and thinking.

20. J. Clauberg, *Elementa philosophiae sive Ontosophia*, now in *Opera Omnia philosophica* [1691], 2 vols.; anastatic reprint (Hildesheim: Olms, 1969).

21. R. Descartes, *Discourse on the Method* (1637), in *Philosophical Writings*, ed. and trans. J. Cottingham, R. Stoothof, and D. Murdoch (Cambridge: Cambridge University Press, 1985), vol. I.

22. In particular, J. Brucker, *Historia critica philosophiae, a mundi incunabilis ad nostram usque aetatem deducta*, Leipzig, 1742–1744, 5 vols.

23. A. G. Baumgarten, *Metaphysica*, cit., and G. F. Meier, *Auszug aus der Vernunftlehre* (Halle, 1752) reprinted in Ak XVII.4 and Ak XVI.3, respectively, with Kant's annotations for lectures.

24. A 832/B 860. On Baumgarten's account, the "architectonic" is the structure of metaphysical knowledge (which Baumgarten regarded as equivalent to "ontology," "metaphysics," and "first philosophy"). On the other hand, Lambert held it to be the art of establishing such a structure.

25. J. Locke, *Essay*, cit., IV, xv.

26. D. Hume, *Treatise*, cit., Book I, Part iii, where this claim is sketched, and more fully presented in the "Abstract" (1740), as also in Sect. IV of the *Enquiry concerning Human Understanding* (1748), ed. P. H. Nidditch (Oxford: Oxford University Press, 1975).

27. We return to this point in Chapter 4.

28.

"That's another thing we've learnt from *your* Nation," said Mein Herr, "map-making. But we've carried it much further than *you*. [. . .] We very soon got to six *yards* to the mile. Then we tried a *hundred* yards to the mile. And then we came to the grandest idea of all! We actually made a map of the country, on the scale of *a mile to the mile*! [. . .] It has never been spread out yet. . . . the farmers objected: they said it would cover the whole country and shut out the sunlight! So now we use the country itself as its own map, and I assure you it does nearly as well." "Sylvie and Bruno Concluded," (1893), chap. 11 in *The Complete Illustrated Works of Lewis Carroll* (London: Chancellor Press, 1993), p. 524.

29. J. McDowell, *Mind and World* (Cambridge: Harvard University Press, 1994); for discussion, I hope I may be forgiven for referring to my "Mente e mondo o scienza ed esperienza?," *Rivista di Estetica*, n. 12 (1999), pp. 3–77.

30. The *Logic* of Jean-Pierre de Crousaz (1663–1750) appeared in 1712 in fully six volumes! What sort of thing could he fill it up with? In fact, it is a treatise on psychology and the theory of discovery and teaches how not to be taken in by prejudices, which is not what would today ordinarily be included in a logic book. We may also recall the eloquent title of the treatise published in London in 1724 by Isaac Watts (1674–1748): *Logick: or, The RIGHT USE of REASON in the Enquiry after TRUTH, with a Variety of RULES to guard against Error in the Affairs of RELIGION and HUMAN LIFE, as well as in the SCIENCES.*

31. E. Cassirer, *Kants Leben und Lehre* (1918) (Darmstadt: Wissenschaftliche Buchgesellschaft, 1977).

32. Cfr. B. Russell, *An Essay on the Foundations of Geometry* (Cambridge: Cambridge University Press, 1897), p. 1:

> Geometry, throughout the 17th and 18th centuries, remained, in the war against empiricism, an impregnable fortress of the idealists. Those who held—as was generally held on the Continent—that certain knowledge, independent of experience, was possible about the real world, had only to point to Geometry: none but a madman, they said, would deny its objective reference. The English Empiricists, in this matter, had, therefore, a somewhat difficult task: either they had to ignore the problem, or if, like Hume and Mill, they ventured on the assault, they were driven into the apparently paradoxical assertion that Geometry, at bottom, had no certainty of a different *kind* from that of Mechanics—only the perpetual presence of spatial impressions, they said, made our experience of the truth of the axioms so wide as to *seem* absolute certainty.

33. See Chapter 11.

34. This is a variability that Hume emphasizes in line with the Cartesian prejudice (that Kant is not concerned to correct), that we ought not to trust the senses because they have sometimes deceived us. See R. Descartes, *Meditations* (1641), in *Philosophical Writings*, cit. II, p. 12.

35. B. Smith, "An Essay on Material Necessity," in P. Hanson and B. Hunter (eds.), *Return of the A Priori* (*Canadian Journal of Philosophy*, Supplementary Vol. 18), 1992.

36. B VIIIff.

37. Kant refers to "intuition" so as to be able to set up a passage between mathematics and Space and Time as pure forms of experience, and this clouds matters somewhat.

38. F. Bacon, *Cogitata et Visa de Interpretatione Naturae, sive De Scientia Operativa* (1607–1609) in *The Works of Francis Bacon*, ed. J. Spedding, R. L. Ellis, D. D. Heath (London: Longmans, 1857), p. 74.

39. This comes out most clearly relative to the thesis about substance, which is at first attributed to physics (B 17) and then to metaphysics (B 795/A 767).

40. I have tried to develop this thought in M. Ferraris, *Il mondo esterno* (Milan: Bompiani, 2001).

41. P. F. Strawson, *Individuals: An Essay in Descriptive Metaphysics* (London: Methuen, 1959); and A. Goldman, *Liaisons: Philosophy Meets the Cognitive and Social Sciences* (Cambridge: MIT Press-Bradford Books, 1992). For an account of the pros and cons of these two approaches (by a partisan of prescriptive metaphysics), see A. C. Varzi, *Parole, oggetti, eventi e altri argomenti di metafisica* (Rome: Carocci, 2001), pp. 28–33.

42. And thus also to confuse epistemology and ontology, on which see Chapter 5.

Chapter 4

1. J. H. Lambert, *Neues Organon oder Gedanken über di Erforschun un Bezeichnung des Wahren und dessen Unterscheidungen von Irrthum und Schein* (1764), 3 vols., ed. G. Schenk (Berlin: Akademie-Verlag, 1990).

2. J. N. Tetens, *Philosophische Versuche über die menschliche Natur und ihre Entwicklung* (1777), 2 vols., anastatic reprint (Hildesheim: Olms, 1979).

3. For Hume (*Treatise*, cit., Book I, Part i, Section I), an idea is a less lively sensation; for Leibniz ("Meditation on Knowledge, Truth and Ideas" in *Philosophical Papers and Letters*, ed. L. E. Loemker (Dordrecht: Reidel, 1969), pp. 291–5, a sensation can be clear and distinct; which is to say that, for both of them, it does not represent something wholly different from a sensible impression.

4. E. Scribano, *L'esistenza di Dio. Storia della prova ontologica da Descartes a Kant* (Rome-Bari: Laterza, 1994).

5. A. Schopenhauer, *The World as Will and Representation* (1819), 2 vols., trans. E. F. J. Payne (New York: Dover, 1958–1969).

6. P. Kitcher, *Kant's Transcendental Psychology* (New York-: Oxford University Press, 1990).

7. A 271/B 326.

8. F. A. Lange, *History of Materialism* (1866), in 2 vols., trans. (in 3 vols.), E. C. Thomas (Boston: Osgood, 1877).

9. A 230–1/B 282–4.

10. J. Barnes, *The Ontological Argument* (London: McMillan, 1972).

11. While for Leibniz, the *res* is what can be distinctly *conceived*, its existence is what can be distinctly *perceived*. "*Res*" can thus be applied to God, to the soul, and to the world (which are never met with in experience, not even the world, which is too big); to the golden mountain (which is not contradictory but happens not to exist); to the square circle (which means something to us, but we are not able to imagine it clearly because it is incoherent); and, as a limiting case, the invention of Italian comedian Walter Chiari, the "Sarchiapone," which, from the description indirectly given, seems to be some sort of animal, though we cannot tell which. In effect, what is excluded is only the Scholastics' "blitiri," the empty and objectless concept, that could be anything and is therefore less than nothing.

12. A 133/B 172.

13. As we have seen, efforts had been made at most to discover a logic that would add to knowledge, but without distinguishing between sensibility and intellect, which was a temptation that Kant sternly frowned on.

14. A 150ff./B 189ff.

15. A 154ff./B 193ff.

16. "It is impossible for anyone to suppose that the same thing is and is not, as some imagine Heraclitus says." Aristotle, *Metaphysics*, IV, 1005b 23–25, trans. H. Treddenick (Cambridge: Loeb, Harvard University Press, 1933).

17. R. Descartes: "we should attend only to those objects of which our minds seem capable of having certain and indubitable cognition." *Rules for the Direction of the Mind*, rule 2, in *Philosophical Writings*, cit., I, p. 10.

18. I. Kant, *Metaphysical Foundations of Natural Science* (1786), trans. J. Ellington (Indianapolis: Bobbs-Merrill, 1970), Preface.

19. B 14.

20. Kant is rather evasive about the status of the "I." Those of his followers who were primarily interested in psychology transcribed the thesis of the I as a physiology of the intellect, which is pretty surely not what Kant would have approved. The transcendental idealists saw in it the beginnings of a construction of the world starting with the "I," but nor would this approach have had Kant's wholehearted approval. Strawson, on the other hand, sees it as a collection of minimum requirements for there to be experience, which is an account of the matter that Kant would have recognized, even if some of its workings out (such as the enfolding of Space in Time and Time in the I) seem to give too much away to the idealist interpretation, while others (such as the role given to the thoroughly psychological faculty of the imagination) give nonarbitrary support to the realist interpretation.

21. T. Griffero, "*I sensi di Adamo. Appunti estetico-teosofici sulla corporeità spirituale,*" *Rivista di Estetica*, n.s., 12, 1999.

22. W. V. O. Quine, "Two Dogmas of Empiricism," *The Philosophical Review*, 60 (1951), pp. 20–43.

23. F. A. Trendelenburg, *Logische Untersuchungen* (1840), 2 vols., 3rd enlarged ed. (Leipzig: Hirzel, 1870).

Chapter 5

1. *Rezensionen zur Kantischen Philosophie 1781–87*, ed. A. Landau (Bebra: Landau Verlag, 1991).

2. R. Ciafardone, *La Critica della ragion pura. Introduzione alla lettura*, cit.

3. Kant complains that the reviewers of the *Critique of Pure Reason* behaved much as someone who, never having seen or heard anything of geometry, were to find a copy of Euclid's *Elements* and to describe it as follows: "The book is a systematic instruction in drawing: the author uses a special language in order to give obscure, unintelligible precepts which are able to achieve nothing more in the end that what anybody could bring about by means of a good eye etc." (*Prolegomena*, trans. cit., p. 145).

4. See F. H. Jacobi, *David Hume on Faith, or Idealism and Realism* (1787) in ed. and trans. G. di Giovanni, *F. H. Jacobi: The Main Philosophical Writings and the Novel Allwill*, (Montreal: McGill-Queen's University Press, 1994), 253–338.

5. J. H. Hamann, *Metakritik ueber den Purismum der Vernunft* (1800), in *Sämtliche Werke* (6 vols.), J. Nadler (Vienna: Herder, 1949–1957); J. H. Herder, *Verstand und Erfahrung. Eine Metakritik zur Kritik der reinen Vernunft*, Part One;

Vernunft und Sprache. Eine Metakritik zur Kritik der reinen Vernunft, Part Two (1799); *Kalligone* (1800), in *Werke*, ed. G. Arnold et al., Frankfurt/M. Deutscher Klassiker Verlag, 10 vols., vol. VIII, 1998, pp. 303–964.

6. We return to this point in Chapter 11.

7. In 1904, the year of the first centenary of Kant's death, the great French mathematician Louis Couturat (1868–1914) wrote an essay that had fun showing that not a single mathematical proposition is synthetic and that all can be resolved by analysis; see L. Couturat, "La philosophie des mathématiques de Kant," *Revue de Métaphysique et de Morale*, XII, 1904, pp. 321–83. The essay carries as its motto a quotation by Zimmermann: "If the judgments of mathematics are synthetic, then the whole of Kant's critique of reason crumbles." The analytic nature of mathematics was then the dominant doctrine (see A. N. Whitehead and B. Russell, *Principia Mathematica* [Cambridge: Cambridge University Press, 1910], 3 vols.), though that would soon change.

8. J. F. Herbart, *Allegemeine Metaphysik* (2 vols.), Königsberg, 1828–9.

9. J. F. Fries, *Neue oder anthropologische Kritik der Vernunft* (1807), reprint of the 2nd (1828) ed. (Berlin: Irmer, 1935).

10. V. Verra, *Costruzione, scienza e filosofia*, in *Romanticismo, esistenzialismo, ontologia della libertà* (Milan: Mursia, 1979), pp. 120–36.

11. On August 7, 1799, Kant distanced himself from Fichte's *Wissenschaftslehre* (*Science of Knowledge*, trans. P. Heath and J. Lachs [Cambridge: Cambridge University Press, 1982]), saying that "a doctrine of science is neither more nor less than mere *logic*, which, with its own principles, does not reach the materials of knowledge" and, a little further on, he quotes the proverb, "God preserve me from my friends, while I shall preserve myself from my enemies" (Ak XII.3, pp. 396–7).

12. E. A. Poe, "The Purloined Letter" (1845), many times reprinted, e.g., in *Complete Tales and Poems* (Harmondsworth: Penguin, 1982), pp. 208–22.

13. Of course, even in Kant's day, there were those who doubted of the telescope and the microscope, defending the unaided human senses as quite sufficient. Nevertheless, a passage like the following is only conceivable in the twentieth century:

> there are duplicates of every object about me—two tables, two chairs, two pens [. . .] One of them has been familiar to me from earliest years. It is a commonplace object of that world which I call the world. How shall I describe it? It has extension; it is comparatively permanent; it is coloured; above all it is *substantial*. By substantial I do not merely mean that it does not collapse when I lean upon it; I mean that it is constituted of "substance" and by that word I am trying to convey to you some conception of its intrinsic nature [. . .] Table No. 2 is my scientific table. It is a more recent acquaintance and I do not feel familiar with it. [. . .] My scientific table is mostly emptiness. Sparsely scattered in that emptiness are numerous electric charges rushing about with great

speed; but their combined bulk amounts to less than a billionth of the
bulk of the table itself. Notwithstanding its strange construction it turns
out to be an entirely efficient table. It supports my writing paper as
satisfactorily as table No. 1; for when I lay the paper on it the electrical
particles with their headlong speed keep hitting the underside so that
the paper is maintained in shuttlecock fashion at a nearly steady level.

Sir Arthur Eddington, *The Nature of the Physical World* (Cambridge: Cambridge University Press, 1929), pp. xi–xii.

14. F. Dretske (*Seeing and Knowing* [Chicago: University of Chicago Press,
1969]) proposes a distinction between "simple seeing" and "epistemic seeing";
R. Casati and A. C. Varzi ("Un altro mondo?," *Rivista di Estetica*, n.s., 19, 2002,
pp. 131–59) distinguish between a "referential function" and an "attributive function." The point is always the same: we can have even complex experiences
without having full competence, much as we can use a hand, a computer or a
lift without knowing how it works.

15. What comes of it is a metaphysics that confuses what we know with
the experience we have of it, making the mistake that modern psychologists
call the "stimulus error." U. Savardi and I. Bianchi (eds.), *Gli errori dello stimolo*
(Verona: CIERRE, 1999). The "possibility conditions" here are systematically
cognitive resources, both in that they concern our forms of knowledge and that
they are indissolubly connected to what we know about things.

16. We may also bear in mind the sentence in §75 della *Critique of Judgment*, according to which there could never be a Newton who was in a position
to unveil the reasons why a blade of grass grows, and which seems to be pretty
straightforwardly falsified by the discovery of DNA.

17. J. R. Searle, *The Construction of Social Reality* (Harmondsworth: Penguin,
1995), pp. 127ff.

18. This is a long-standing tradition, which begins with the attack against
empiricism launched by the Common Sense philosophers (above all, Thomas
Reid, 1710–1796), and continues with the naive realism of G. E. Moore; see his
"Defence of Common Sense" (1925) in his *Philosophical Papers* (London: George
Allen and Unwin, 1959), pp. 32–59.

19. J. R. Searle, *The Construction of Social Reality*, cit., pp. 7–13. As regards
epistemology (what is known), we can have *subjective* claims like "Rembrandt
is better than Rubens," where the proposition refers to something I *know* and
declares a personal preference, as well as *objective* ones like "In 1632 Rembrandt
lived in Amsterdam," where the proposition refers to something I *know*, but
does not declare a personal preference. Also as regards ontology (what is), we
have *subjective* claims like "My right hand hurts," where the proposition refers to
something that, epistemically, I *have* as a subject, but that constitutes an objective
fact, if it is true that my right hand hurts, as well as *objective* ones such as "Ben
Nevis is higher than Snowdon," where the *subjective* one might be "Ben Nevis
is more beautiful than Snowdon." It is not hard to see that there is a difference

of level here. "My right hand hurts," which is ontologically subjective, given that it is me who has the pain, is epistemologically objective if it really does hurt.

20. *Il mondo esterno*, cit.

21. O. Lipmann, "Das Wesen der naiven Physik. Grundsätze einer Prüfung der Fähigkeit zu intelligentem physischen Handeln," in O. Lipmann and H. Bogen (eds.), *Naive Physik. Theoretische und experimentelle Untersuchungen über die Fähigkeit zu intelligentem Handeln*, Arbeiten aus dem Institut für angewandte Psychologie in Berlin (Leipzig: Barth, 1923). The most mature exposition of this approach is to be found in P. Bozzi, *Fisica ingenua* (Milan: Garzanti, 1990). The philosophical presuppositions are examined in R. Casati and B. Smith, "Naive Physics: An Essay in Ontology," *Philosophical Psychology*, 7/2 (1994), pp. 225–44.

Chapter 6

1. R. Descartes, *Meditations* II, in *Philosophical Writings*, cit. II, pp. 20–3.

2. J. Locke, *Essay*, cit., Book IV, Chapter xv.

3. Which has been put under pressure by D. Davidson, "On the Very Idea of a Conceptual Scheme" (1974) in his *Inquiries into Truth and Interpretation* (Oxford: Basil Blackwell, 1984), pp. 183–98, with the argument that what we have here is a surviving dogma of empiricism resting on the untenable distinction between scheme (which belongs to the mind) and content (which belongs to experience). Our present strategy, however, is rather different and seeks to defend the autonomy of content relative to scheme, where this latter is basically epistemological.

4. G. Kanisza, *Organisations of Vision: Essays on Gestalt Perception* (New York, 1979).

5. This dependence implies that the world is the result of a construction of the "I," which, in the limiting case, is the owner of the universe, with a point of view that, after Kant, developed into the idea of the omnipotence of history and of society in constructing the world.

6. See the discussion of space in Chapter 7.

7. R. Gregory, *The Intelligent Eye* (London, 1970).

8. E. H. Gombrich, *Art and Illusion* (London: Phaidon, 1960), pp. 60–3.

9. C. E. von Hoften and E. S. Spelke, "Object Perception and Object-Directed Reaching in Infancy," *Journal of Experimental Psychology. General*, 114 (1985), pp. 198–211.

10. It should be noted that the schema that babies a few months old have does not correspond closely to the Kantian schema of "substance."

11. Cf. F. C. Bartlett, *Remembering: A Study in Experimental and Social Psychology* (Cambridge: Cambridge University Press, 1932); also J. J. Gibson, *The Perception of the Visual World* (Cambridge: Cambridge University Press, 1950).

12. See U. Eco, *Kant and the Platypus*, trans. A. McEwen (London: Secker and Warburg, 1999). For development of the point, see my "Il problema non è l'ornitorinco. È Kant" in my *Il mondo esterno*, (Milan: Bompiani, 2001), pp. 27–85.

13. F. Kafka, "The Cares of a Family Man," trans. W. and E. Muir, in *The Complete Short Stories of Franz Kafka*, ed. N. H. Glatzer (1983) (London: Vintage, 1999), p. 428.

14. See F. Nietzsche, *Writings from the Late Notebooks*, ed. R. Bittner, trans. K. Sturge (Cambridge: Cambridge University Press, 2003).

15. This point has been the object of much discussion by philosophers over the last twenty years in the wake of G. Evans, *The Varieties of Reference* (Oxford: Oxford University Press, 1982). See J. Bermúdez, *the Paradox of Self-Consciousness* (Cambridge: MIT Press, 1998), esp. Chapter 3.

16. The point here, however, is not the claim that "intuitions without concepts are blind," as Kant understands it, but rather the well-known question raised by the Irish natural philosopher William Molyneux (1656–1698). As expressed in his letter to Locke of March 2, 1693, Molyneux's "jocose problem" runs as follows: "Suppose a man born blind, and now adult, and taught by his touch to distinguish between a cube and a sphere (suppose) of ivory, nighly of the same bigness, so as to tell when he felt one and t'other, which is the cube, which the sphere. Suppose then the cube and the sphere placed on a table, and the blind man to me made to see; query, Whether by his sight, before he touched them, he could distinguish and tell, which is the globe, which the cube?" (in *The Works of John Locke* [9 vols., ed. 1794], anastatic reprint with intro. J. Yolton [London: Routledge-Thoemmes, 1997], VIII, p. 311). Molyneux's own response to the puzzle is to say, "I answer not; for though he has obtained experience of how a globe, and how a cube affects his touch; yet he has not yet attained the experience, that what affects his touch so or so, must affect his sight so or so; or that a protuberant angle in the cube, that pressed his hand unequally, shall appear to his eye as it does in the cub" (loc. cit.). Though Locke does not pronounce on the matter in his reply to this letter (of March 28, 1693), in the second edition of the *Essay* (1694) he paraphrases Molyneux's query and expresses tentative agreement with his diagnosis of the situation (II, ix, 8). For a review of the solutions that have been proposed down though the centuries and an account of how contemporary science views the matter, see A. Jacomuzzi et al., "Molyneux's Problem Redux," *Journal of the History of the Behavioral Sciences*, 2 (2003).

17. In *Der Logik der Philosophie* (1911, in *Gesammelte Schriften*, Tübingen, Mohr, 1923, II, p. 74), the German philosopher Emile Lask (1875–1915) had proposed reformulating the Kantian way of putting the matter in the following terms: "Form without content is empty, content without form is naked." The nakedness must have attracted the attention of Edmund Husserl because, years later, in *Experience and Judgment* (1938, trans. J. S Churchill and K. Ameriks [Evanston, IL: Northwestern University Press, 1973]), he writes that judgment is a *garment* of ideas projected onto the world of intuition. This amounts to saying that logical form is superimposed, like cloak, on a world that is through-and-through structured like a body.

18. L. Wittgenstein, *Philosophical Investigations*, trans. G. E. M. Anscombe (Oxford: Basil Blackwell, 1953).

19. This is the spirit of the argument elaborated, for instance, by Příhonský (*Neuer Anti-Kant*, cit., p. 25), who reasoned as follows: (1) Kant has problems with the notion of "causality," which for him is a priori (we do not learn it from experience, inasmuch as it forms part of the gifts of the pure "I"), yet it needs experience at least as input (if there were no causation in the world, the pure concept of causality would not be activated). (2) If, on the other hand, we say that causality is an exclusively conceptual notion, the whole business of the "I" that applies its pure concepts to the objects of experience becomes secondary, "because to say that a thing *changes* means only that it possesses at different moments different and mutually exclusive properties. On that basis, the concept of 'change' involves nothing that is not conceptual: substance, property, time and so on. It is therefore composed only of pure concepts and does not include a single empirical representation or intuition." We return to the question of objectivity independent of thought in Chapter 11.

20. B 69–70, with slight changes to Kemp Smith, who puts the second sentence of this passage in square brackets to indicate that, as he says in the note added, it "conflicts with the main argument, and is probably a later addition carelessly inserted."

21. When, for instance, in cases of carbon monoxide poisoning, the mechanisms of chromatic constancy do not work, subjects perceive the colors' wavelengths and not the chromatic stability of the ecological environment. If you look at the series of Monet's paintings of Rouen Cathedral, the idea will become clear. Is this, nevertheless, grounds enough to claim that colors are in the eye or in the brain? Obviously not. And that for *logical* reasons: color is conceptually in the thing, and hence it is a conceptual error to deny it. A parallel case would be that of numbers: their psychological origin does not explain their status.

22. This is, of course, possible come what may, but the cost is a drastically corrective metaphysics.

23. A 100–101.

Chapter 7

1. I. Kant, *De mundi sensibilis atque intelligibilis forma et principiis* (1770).

2. P. F. Strawson, *The Bounds of Sense*, cit., pp. 47ff.

3. As we have seen, there is a fourth point that Kant does not set himself to demonstrate because he takes it to be obvious, namely that space is identical with *Euclidean geometry* (which he announces explicitly) and that time is identical with *elementary arithmetic* (which he assumes tacitly).

4. C. Stumpf, "Psychologie und Erkenntnistheorie," *Kaiserliche Bayeriche Akademie der Wissenschaften*, I Kl. Vol. xix, Section II (1891).

5. For development, I refer the reader to my "Lo strano caso degli opposti incongruenti," in *Rivista di estetica*, n.s., 11 (2/1999), pp. 39–52. An English account of the Kantian passages may be found in C. D. Broad, *Kant:*

An Introduction, ed. C. Lewy (Cambridge: Cambridge University Press, 1978), pp. 37–44.

6. During World War II, the American psychologist J. J. Gibson (1904–1979) was working for the Air Force to try to find a way of preventing accidents during landing, in which trainee pilots flew into the ground as if they were continuing the flight trajectory. How could this be? As Gibson learned, aerial space is very different from terrestrial space, and the young pilots were unable to form a unitary concept of it, with catastrophic results (see J. J. Gibson, *The Ecological Approach to Visual Perception* [New York: Houghton Mifflin, 1979]).

7. C. Becchio, *Ragionamento deduttivo e spazialità. Un'ipotesi sperimentale e alcune considerazioni filosofiche*, PhD diss. in aesthetics, University of Turin, academic year 1999–2000.

8. "For when we are aware of movement we are thereby aware of time, since even if it were dark and we were conscious of no bodily movement, but something were 'going on' in our minds, we should, from that very experience, recognise the passage of time." Aristotle, *Physics*, IV xi, 219a3–6, trans. P. H. Wicksteed and F. M. Cornford (Cambridge: Loeb, Harvard University Press, 1957).

9. B 275ff. The argument is not very strong. Kant's idea is that, given that the "I" perceives itself as a temporal flow, there must be something at rest outside it, namely the external world, relative to which the "I" feels itself to be flowing. But any train journey will put the principle in doubt: the train may be in movement while it is still in the station (in Kantian terms, inside rather than outside), or one can have the impression of being at rest while moving at the same speed as another train traveling in the same direction.

Chapter 8

1. This concept of time is much praised by Heidegger in his book on Kant of 1929 (*Kant and the Problem of Metaphysics*, cit.), but the virtues that Heidegger sees in it from an existentialist point of view, that is, from the viewpoint of hypertranscendentalism (the world is at the disposal of man), can turn into the equal and opposite defects.

2. A 320/B 377.

3. Leibniz, "Meditations on knowledge, truth and ideas," in Loemker (ed.) cit.

4. F. Brentano, *Psychology from an Empirical Standpoint* (1874), trans. A. C. Rancurello et al. (London: Routledge, 1969), 2nd ed., 1995, Book ii, chap. I, §5.

5. J. Locke, *Essay*, IV, ii, 14:

> I ask any one, Whether he be not invincibly conscious to himself of a different Perception, when he looks on the Sun by day, or smells a Rose, or only thinks on that Savour, or Odour? We as plainly find

the difference there is between any *Idea* revived in our Minds by our own Memory, and actually coming into our Minds by our Senses, as we do between any two distinct *Ideas*. If any one say, a Dream may do the same thing, and all these *Ideas* may be produced in us without any external Objects, he may please to dream that I make him this Answer, 1. That 'tis no great matter, whether I remove his Scruple or not: Where all is but Dream, Reasoning and Arguments are of no use, Truth and Knowledge nothing. 2. That I believe he will allow a very manifest difference between dreaming of being in the Fire, and actually being in it. But yet if he be resolved to appear so sceptical, as to maintain, that what I call actually being in the Fire, is nothing but a Dream; and that we cannot thereby certainly know, that any such thing as Fire actually exists without us: I answer, That we certainly finding, that Pleasure or Pain follows upon the application of certain Objects to us, whose Existence we perceive, or dream that we perceive, by our Senses, this certainty is as great as our Happiness, or Misery, beyond which, we have no concernment to know, or to be.

6. Plato, *Republic*, 597ff. The point is also made by Gibson, *The Ecological Approach to Visual Perception*, cit.

7. It seems to me that this resistance, which I call "unemendability" in my book *Il mondo esterno*, is important. While I am looking at a fire, I may think of it as a process of oxydation, as the action of phlogiston and caloric; but, under normal conditions, I cannot put my hand into it and not get burned. To do otherwise would be playing with fire. Images too are subject to certain constraints (no color without extension, no sound without duration). As Descartes noted, even the most extravagant painter's inventions or images in dreams follow the rules of representation (*Meditations*, I, trans. cit., II, p. 13). One might therefore think that unemendability is not a criterion for distinguishing things from images, but the fact remains that images are much more malleable than objects.

8. I can think of a triangle; but if I ask myself how long the sides are, I can reply one-and-a-half centimeters, fifteen centimeters, or fifteen meters, if I imagine it some way off. The mental image of the Turin-Milan motorway is not 126 kilometers long and does not last two hours.

9. W. James, *Principles of Psychology* (1890) (2 vols.) (New York: Dover, 1950), chap. XVIII.

10. T. Reid, *Essays on the Intellectual Powers*, cit.

11. A. Schopenhauer, *The World as Will and Representation* (1819), §5: "Life and dreams are pages from the same book. Real life is reading without interruption. But when the normal moment for reading (daytime) is over and the time comes for rest, we often continue idly to flick over the pages, opening the book here and there, without order or sequence, sometimes running into a page we have already read and sometimes into one that is new, but the book we are reading is always the same."

12. M. Merleau-Ponty, *The Visible and the Invisible*, (1964), ed. C. Lefort, trans. A. Lingis (Evanston, IL: Northwestern University Press, 1968), p. 7: "The binocular perception is not made up of two monocular perceptions surmounted, it is of another order. The monocular images *are* not in the same sense that the thing perceived with both eyes *is*. They are phantoms and it is the real; they are pre-things and it is the thing."

13. The present account of "substance" and "cause" summarizes the discussion in my *Il mondo esterno*, cit., pp. 71–82.

14. R. Casati and A. C. Varzi, *Buchi e altre superficialità* (Milan, Garzanti, 1996).

15. Kant might reply that the distinction is not based on time, and that accidents are in general a higher order of object than substances. Except that we can find no trace of such an approach in the way he sets things up and in his exclusive insistence on temporal duration.

16. "Rock, soil, sand, mud, clay, oil, tar, wood, minerals, metal, and above all, the various tissues of plants and animals are examples of environmental substances. Each of these has a more or less specific composition, but almost none is a chemical compound, a pure chemical of the sort that is found on the shelves of chemistry laboratories" J. J. Gibson, *The Ecological Approach to Visual Perception* (Boston: Houghton Mifflin, 1979), pp. 19–20.

17. We might recall that Descartes's fiddling with the wax in *Meditations* II was made possible, in a nonaccidental way, by the fact of there being only one word for wax, liquid, and solid, unlike the case of water, ice, and steam.

18. P. F. Strawson, *Bounds of Sense*, cit., p. 133ff.

19. On another occasion, at nightfall, he slapped a colleague on the back just as the streetlamps were coming on, giving the effect of having lit them himself, with his colleague as the switch.

20. Once, during an earthquake, a fellow who was playing cards played his hand with great force and ended up on the floor below: his very first impression was of having smashed through the floor with his fist on the table.

21. A. Michotte, *La perception de la causalité* (Louvain: Institut Supérieur de Philosophie, 1946).

Chapter 9

1. As he maintains in the *Critique of Pure Reason*, when he says, for instance, that *experience* is possible only thought the representation of a necessary connection of perception (B 218). But, as we have seen, the identity between science and experience lies at the heart of the Copernican Revolution and of Transcendental Fallacy.

2. As he points out in the preface to the *Metaphysical Foundation of Natural Science*, cit. (Ak IV, p. 467ff.), thus weakening his claim.

3. For the reader of Italian, there is an excellent presentation of the metaphysical deduction in S. Marcucci, *Guida alla lettura della Critica della ragion pura di Kant*, cit., pp. 72–86.

4. J. L. Borges, "The Analytical Language of John Wilkins."

5. It was an enterprise worthy of an acute thinker like Aristotle to make search for these fundamental concepts. But as he did so on no principle, but merely picked them up as he came by them, and at first procured ten of them, which he called *categories* (predicaments). Afterward he believed he had discovered five others, which he added under the name of post-predicaments. But his table still remained defective. Besides there are to be found some modes of pure sensibility (*quando, ubi, situs*, also *prius, simul*) and an empirical concept (*motus*), none of which has any place in a table of the concepts that trace their origin to the understanding. Aristotle's list also enumerates among the original concepts some derivative concepts (*actio, passio*); and of the original concepts some are entirely lacking. B 107/A 81.

6. B 97/A 72.

7. P. F. Strawson, *Bounds of Sense*, cit., p. 74

8. What we have here is an explanation of knowledge with a classical lineage, going back in outline to Plato's *Theaetetus*.

9. This comes out in the passage on the cinnabar to which we referred earlier: "If cinnabar were sometimes red, sometimes black, sometimes light, sometimes heavy [. . .] my empirical imagination could never find opportunity when representing red color to bring to mind heavy cinnabar" (A 100–1).

10. A 97.

11. Which would perhaps explain the behavior of animals (animals interact in the world but do not have categories, which is a sign that the world is organized on its own account), but it is unclear how it should not suffice to explain human behavior, if, for all his rationalism, the tolerant Leibniz is right in thinking that men act without reasoning, just like animals 90 percent of the time, while Kant sees reason at work in 100 percent of our interactions.

12. "In so far as imagination is spontaneity, I sometimes also entitle it the *productive* imagination" (B 152). This is a point to which we return shortly.

13. G. Berkeley, *Treatise on the Principles of Human Knowledge* (1710), §§10–17.

14. P. F. Strawson, *Bounds of Sense*, cit., p. 77.

15. A 141/B 180.

16. A 569–70/B 597–8.

17. U. Eco, M. Ferraris, and D. Marconi, "Lo schema del cane," *Rivista di Estetica*, n.s., 8, 1998, pp. 3–27.

18. See, further, Chapter 10.

19. A 144–5/B 183–5.

20. In the *Opus postumum* (1796–1803), Kant writes, "Concluding the particular (*in concreto*) from the universal (*in abstracto*), or rather the singular from

mere concepts, and to everything else from that, is a self-delusion." But in that very text, as illustrated by the thematic selection of the English edition (ed. E. Förster, trans. E. Förster and M. Rosen [Cambridge: Cambridge University Press, 1993]), Kant engages in a repeated search for the elusive North-West Passage that will give him access, by way of the concepts, to the schemata that are able to anticipate experience "insofar as it is material" (as he puts it, *quoad materiale*), which is to say, precisely down to the level of the individual.

21. Where 7 and 5 would be substances, if we apply the other paradigm of the synthetic a priori judgment, reciprocal action will show itself in the fact that, unless I put the addition sign between the 7 and the 5, they remain as they were and causality would be the law according to which, if I put in the addition sign, I get 12.

22. In the *Physics*, Aristotle had already compared the instant to a point and time to a line; Kant is right to insist on the powerful intuitiveness of this way of representing the thing.

23. I discuss them shortly.

24. A 33/B 49–50, B 154, B 156.

25. A 162–4/B 203–4.

26. B 137–8.

27. C. Stumpf, "Psychologie und Erkenntnistheorie," cit.

28. In his *Competenza lessicale* (Rome-Bari: Laterza, 1999), Diego Marconi has brought out the usefulness of the schema as a "method of construction" with clear reference of Kant, but also making use of the result of cognitive science. But we should not forget that Kant keeps to the level of hypothesis, and, moreover, that special feature of his camera is the transcendental imagination, which not only is an extravagance, but also gave rise to even more outrageous extravagances, from idealism onward. In the late jottings collected under the title *Opus postumum* (1796–1803, in Ak. Vols. XXI and XXII), Kant tries to make plain the mystery of the imagination by hypothesizing a no less mysterious element, the "ether," which is a "sensible object, that nevertheless, like space, does not strike the senses, but only reason," "it is a hypothetical thing, to which reason must appeal to arrive at the supreme foundation of the corporeal world." On the problem of the imagination, I hope I may be forgiven for referring the reader to my "Origini della immaginazione trascendentale," in *Annuario filosofico*, 10 (Milan: Mursia, 1994), pp. 133–226.

29. P. Bozzi, *Fenomenologia sperimentale* (Bologna: Il Mulino, 1989), p. 52.

Chapter 10

1. D. C. Dennett, *The Intentional Stance* (Cambridge: MIT Press, 1987).

2. G. Lakoff and M. Johnson, *Philosophy in the Flesh. The Embodied Mind and Its Challenge to Western Thought* (New York: Basic Books, 1999).

3. But nor was it so to his contemporaries, if we put to one side the Leibnizians, who, as we have seen, had other fish to fry.

4. See. A. Reinach, *The Apriori Foundations of the Civil Law* (1913), trans. in *Aletheia* 3 (1983), pp. 1–142.

5. I. Kant, *Critique of Judgment* (1790), trans. cit., §6 (Ak V, pp. 211–12).

6. I. Kant, *Critique of Judgment*, §61 (Ak V, pp. 359–61). The example of the eye and the appeal to teleology is already in Leibniz's *Discourse on Metaphysics* (1686) §19 (trans. in Loemker (ed.), cit., pp. 315–16). One of the founders of modern cognitivism, David Marr puts the point as follows: "trying to understand perception by studying only neurons is like trying to understand bird flight by studying only feathers. It just cannot be done. In order to understand bird flight, we have to understand aerodynamics; only then do the structure of feathers and the different shapes of birds' wings make sense" (*Vision* [San Francisco: Freeman, 1982], p. 27). The role of intentionality (understood as "teleology") in the explanation of reality has been given its due by Dennett in *The Intentional Stance*, cit. The example that strikes us as both most expressive and most amusing of this is the following.

> The procedure is in fact very simple. First, the things are divided into various groups. Obviously, each pile depends on how much there is to do. If the means are lacking, we pass to the next phase, otherwise all is well. It is important not to exaggerate. In other words, it is better to do a few things at a time than too many. In the short term, this may not seem important, but complications can easily arise and mistakes can be costly. To begin with, the procedure may seem complicated, but soon it will be just another of the many aspects of everyday life. It is unlikely that, in the near future, there will no longer be need of it, but one can never tell. Once the procedure has been carried out, the things can be put back in various groups and returned to their places. In the end, we shall have to take them up again and repeat the whole cycle. But this is part of our life.

Unless you know the objective of all this, you cannot guess that what is being described is doing the washing; adapted from J. D. Bransford and M. K. Johnson, "Consideration of some problems of comprehension," W. G. Chase (ed.), *Visual Information Processing* (New York: Academic, 1973).

7. I. Kant, *Critique of Judgment*, trans. cit., §67 (Ak V, p. 378).

Chapter 11

1. For a brief history of the reception of Kant, see. A. Guerra, *Introduzione a Kant*, cit. (updated to 1997 by G. Gigliotti), pp. 220–30. For a history of transcendentalism G. Gilgliotti, *Avventure e disavventure del trascendentale* (Naples: Guida, 1989).

2. R. Rorty (ed.), *The Linguistic Turn* (Chicago: Chicago University Press, 1967).

3. H. Putnam, *Mind, Language and Reality* (Cambridge: Cambridge University Press, 1975).

4. "You know, I know that this steak doesn't exist. I know that when I put it in my mouth, the Matrix is telling my brain that it is juicy and delicious. After nine years, you know what I realise: ignorance is bliss" (Cypher in *The Matrix*, 1999).

5. T. Nagel, "What Is It Like to be a Bat?," *Philosophical Review*, 83 (1974), pp. 435–50; reprinted in his *Mortal Questions* (Cambridge: Cambridge University Press, 1979), pp. 165–80.

6. A. Schopenhauer, *The World as Will and Representation* (1819), cit., §1: "'The world is my representation': here is a truth that holds for every living and thinking being."

7. I. Kant, *Critique of Practical Reason* (1788), trans T. K. Abbott (London: Longmans, 1909), §§I–IX, pp. 244–6 (Ak V, pp. 146–8).

8. A. Meinong, *On the Theory of Objects* (1904), trans. I. Levi, D. B. Terrell, and R. M. Chisholm, in R. M. Chisholm (ed.), *Realism and the Background of Phenomenology* (New York: The Free Press, 1960).

9. J. R. Searle, *The Construction of Social Reality* (Harmondsworth: Penguin, 1995), p. 3.

10. G. Frege, "Thoughts" (1918), trans. P.T. Geach and R. H. Stoothof, in Frege, *Logical Investigations* (Oxford: Basil Blackwell, 1977), pp. 1–30.

11. G. Berkeley, *Principles*, cit. The argument is very subtle and can easily lead to skeptical outcomes, as can be seen in the very first lines of Giovanni Gentile's *Teoria generale dello spirito come atto puro* (1916), in G. Gentile, *Opere filosofiche*, ed. E. Garin (Milan: Garzanti, 1991), p. 459: "From the beginning of the eighteenth century, with the doctrine of George Berkeley, the following idea comes to the fore: that reality cannot be thought except in relation to the activity of thinking, on which grounds it is thinkable, and in relation to which it is not just a possible object, but the real or actual object of knowledge. The mode of conceiving of a reality is in the first instance the mind in which this reality is represented; therefore the concept of material reality is absurd."

12. B 274–5.

13. A 190ff./B 236ff.

14. This line of thought was already proposed as part of his anti-empiricist polemic by Thomas Reid in *Inquiry into the Human Mind* (1764), cit.

15. The splendid thing is that Kant discusses the case, along with the question of the incongruent opposites, in the *Metaphysical Foundations of Natural Science*, cit., but without seeming to see the problematic consequences of either for his own theory.

16. I. Kant, *Critique of Practical Reason*, cit., I, I, I, §7, trans. cit., pp. 120–1.

17. This seems to be the presupposition of Steven Spielberg's *Minority Report* (2002). And from it we can draw some embarrassing consequences, such as Kant's firm support for the death penalty on the grounds roughly that, if one is innocent, it is not so bad (because one is at peace with one's conscience), whereas it is absolutely just for the guilty (who, being wicked, will give more

weight to life than to honor); see *The Metaphysic of Morals*, trans. M. J. Gregor (Cambridge: Cambridge University Press, 1991), "Doctrine of Right," 49 E. It is worth citing what Kant says at length:

> Supposing that—to take the case of the latest Scottish rebellion, in which many (such as *Balmerino* and others) believed themselves, by taking part in it, to be doing their duty towards the House of *Stuart*, while others acted only out of personal considerations—the House of Lords had decided that each should have the freedom to choose between death and forced labour; I say that the man of honour would prefer death, while the low man would choose forced labour, because this is how the nature of the human spirit behaves. And this is because the former is acquainted with something that he esteems and appreciates more even that life itself, namely *honour*, while the latter will always regard life, even full of shame, as preferable to not being alive at all [. . .] Now, the former man is incontestably less deserving of punishment than the latter, so that, by inflicting death equally on both, they are not punished at all proportionately, the former lightly, according to his lights, and the latter, also according to his way of thinking, harshly. If, conversely, both were sentenced to forced labour, the former would be punished too severely and the latter too softly for his lowness. *Death*, therefore, is also in this case, where many criminals are joined in a plot, the best compensation to public justice (Ak VI, pp. 333–4).

18. M. F. Scheler, *Formalism in Ethics and Non-Formal Ethics of* (1912), trans. M. S. Frings and R. Funk (Evanston, IL: Northwestern University Press, 1973).

19. J. A. Coffa, *The Semantic Tradition from Kant to Carnap* (Cambridge: Cambridge University Press, 1991).

20. B. Bolzano, *Wissenschaftslehre. Versuche einer ausfürhlichen und größtentheils neuen Darstellung der Logik mit steter Rücksicht auf deren bisherige Bearbeiter* (Sulzbach, 1837).

21. F. Příhonský, *Neuer Anti-Kant*, cit.

22. A. Meinong, *Theory of Objects*, cit.

23. G. Frege, "Thoughts," cit.

24. A sentence like "Mickey Mouse is nastier than Donald Duck" turns out to be very hard to justify, because Mickey Mouse and Donald Duck do not exist in space and time, and pictures of them as such are neither nice nor nasty.

25. E. Husserl, *Logical Investigations* (1900–1901), trans. J. N. Findlay (London: Routledge); and Kegan Paul, 1970, Third Investigation; on which see M. Barale, "Postfazione: Per una lettura di Husserl e Kant," in the Italian translation of E. Husserl, *Kant e l'idea della fenomenologia trascendentale (1923/24)*, by C. La Rocca (Milan: Il Saggiatore, 1990), pp. 197–245.

26. F. Kafka, "The Trees," in *Complete Short Stories*, cit., p. 382.

Index

Superman, 45
Swedenborg, E., 10
synthetic *a priori*, 34, 38–41, 126n21

Taddio, L., 333*n*40
Talleyrand (C.M. de Talleyrand-
    Périgord), 101
teleology, 11, 93, 94, 127n6
Tetens, J.N., 35, 115n2
thalers (100), 34, 36–7, 88, 105,
    111n10
thing in itself (noumenon), 34–5, 57,
    93, 95, 99, 100
"thoughts without content are empty,"
    4, 17
time, 3, 5, 10, 14, 16–18, 26–8, 36,
    39–41, 57, 61, 63–5, 67, 71–2,
    82, 84–8, 99, 101, 104, 110n10,
    112n16, 114n37, 116n20, 121n3,
    122nn8–9, 122n1
Tonally, G., 109n12
transcendental aesthetic, 61–2

transcendental fallacy, 30, 38, 43–7,
    49, 79, 80, 124n1
Trendelenburg, F.A., 116n 23
Trier, L. von, 102

unemendability, 123n7
unity of consciousness (apperception),
    14, 34, 40, 65, 68, 81, 86

Vanzetti, B., 107n2
Varzi, A.C., 111n4, 114n41, 118n14,
    124n14
Verra, V., 117n10
Voltaire, (F.M. Arouet), 9, 94
von Hoften, C.E., 119n9

Wasianski, E.A.C., 108n2
Watts, I., 113n30
Whitehead, A.N., 117n7
Wittgenstein, L., 120n18
Wolff, C., 21, 24, 25, 26, 27, 112n10

Yates, F., 108n7